SURVIVAL OF THE FITTEST

SURVIVAL OF THE FITTEST

New Product Development During The 90's

PHILIP A. HIMMELFARB

PRENTICE HALL
Englewood Cliffs, New Jersey 07632

Prentice-Hall International (UK) Limited, *London*
Prentice-Hall of Australia Pty. Limited, *Sidney*
Prentice-Hall Canada, Inc., *Toronto*
Prentice-Hall Hispanoamericana, S.A., *Mexico*
Prentice-Hall of India Private Limited, *New Delhi*
Prentice-Hall of Japan, Inc., *Tokyo*
Simon & Schuster Asia Pte. Ltd., *Singapore*
Editora Prentice-Hall do Brasil, Ltda., *Rio de Janeiro*

10 9 8 7 6 5 4 3 2 1

Library of Congress Cataloging-in-Publication Data

Himmelfarb, Philip A.
  Survival of the fittest : product development during the 1990s /
Philip A. Himmelfarb.
   p.   cm.
  Includes bibliographic references and index.
  ISBN 0-13-879313-1
  1. New products—Management. I. Title.
HF5415.153.H55   1992   92-5114
658.5'75—dc20   CIP

ISBN-0-13-879313-1

PRENTICE HALL
Professional Publishing
Englewood Cliffs, NJ 07632
Simon & Schuster. A Paramount Communications Company

Printed in the United States of America

Table of Contents

Introduction

In 1876, Alexander Graham Bell first demonstrated that people could use electricity to talk to each other over a distance. In 1877, Thomas Edison invented the phonograph. These were followed by a series of other inventions by Americans: black and white television, wire recorders, triode oscillation for radio transmission, the transistor, portable radios, color television, stereophonic transmission of sound, and home videocassette recorders.

These inventions became the basis of the American consumer electronics industry.

Until recently, American industry controlled this business. But, in the last 20 years, the consumer electronics business was lost to the Japanese.

How did it happen that others ran with our technology and dominated the marketplace? How did we give it all away?

The answer is that companies in other countries learned that, while new technology is important, it is nowhere as important as understanding the marketplace and getting products to the market first. They learned that the way to command greater market share is to get new products to the market before anyone else and to follow up with an array of improved products that have more and more features.

And they learned that they had to listen to their customers. When Honda and Toyota wanted the interiors of their cars to be more attractive to their American customers, they went out and asked people what they liked and disliked about instrument clusters and dashboard displays. Detroit automakers didn't do that and were surprised to discover, years later, that people preferred the dashboards of Japanese cars.

A number of U.S. manufacturing companies of all different sizes, large and small, have already learned the importance of fast product development and introduction. Many other U.S. companies have gotten the message and are working hard to make the shift from slow to fast product development.

More and more U.S. executives are waking up to the fact that the survival of their companies will, in large measure, be determined by how fast they can get relevant new products into the marketplace, by how well they can grab and keep market share.

American management is also realizing that, as pressure on earnings intensifies, there will be fewer dollars available for new product development. They are discovering that they will have to learn how to get a bigger bang from each dollar spent.

What will it take for American companies to survive and grow during the next decade and beyond? The answer is clear. They will have to grasp the importance of identification of marketplace needs, fast product development, fast manufacturing start-up, and fast shipping of new products into the marketplace. They will have to develop new management tools and to abandon the old, comfortable, but ineffective, methods of managing new product development.

I decided to write this book because of my increasing concern with the fact that we are such a great nation and we are blessed with such creative minds, yet we have given away so much of our standing in the world marketplace. So many of our companies have insisted on clinging to old methods of managing new product development. I am tired of listening to Japan-bashing by people who fail to place responsibility where it belongs, who fail to believe that we did it to ourselves.

This book is based on the premise that American industry can learn to manage its technological, marketing, and financial resources to achieve a position of excellence in the world marketplace. Just as we are responsible for our problems, we can be responsible for our resurgence as a world power in the marketplace, provided we have techniques for shortening the time it takes to get credible new products into consumer's hands.

The material contained in the following pages is devoted to providing specific tools and techniques that will dramatically speed up the new product development cycle. It is the result of my nearly 30 years of successful product development experience, both in industry and as a consultant and seminar leader. It is designed to help all levels of company management and the people who actually do the work: those who are dedicated to excellence in new product development.

Survival of the Fittest provides a global view of new product development, comparing the slow, phased approach that is so widely practiced with a much faster and more effective multifunctional, parallel team approach. It offers techniques for managing teams and for improving the flow of creative ideas, and it addresses the cultural and other barriers that get in the way. This book deals with the different stages of the product development cycle; the interrelationship of time, quality, and product features; and the need to freeze product features and design specifications early. It also provides specific guidance for senior management.

Many other issues are also addressed in *Survival of the Fittest*, for example, estimating project costs, controlling projects with critical path management, examining lessons from the Japanese, knowing when to kill a development project, and uncovering marketplace needs.

This book contains many checklists that will make the transition to fast new product development much easier. Among the valuable checklists are criteria for selecting and prioritizing projects, a simplified approach to "quality function deployment," ten steps to starting a development project, a 95-question audit of your company's state of new product development readiness, determining whether to kill a development project, sources of ideas for new products, contents of a business plan, characteristics of creative organizations, questions to be asked at every stage of the development cycle, and ground rules for team operation.

Discussions of over 100 companies that have achieved fast new product development are found in this book, including AT&T, Motorola, W. H. Brady, John Deere, Ingersoll-Rand, Honda, Toyota, Matsushita, Sony, 3M, Eaton, and NCR.

ACKNOWLEDGMENTS

I thank the important mentors of my early years: Warren Litsky at the University of Massachusetts, Phil Thayer at Arthur D. Little Company, and Virgil Berry at Schlitz Brewing Company. I also thank my wife, Carole, who has stood by me patiently, lovingly, and steadfastly as I have developed my ideas and written this book. My children, Michael, Elana, and Peter, also deserve a big vote of thanks for their uncritical and never-ending devotion to my cause, whatever it might happen to be.

I especially thank my father, David, who shared with me his work ethic and an abounding curiosity about the way things work. He wrote his first book, a manual on cordage manufacturing technology, when he was in his early fifties. I am pleased to be following in his footsteps.

1 New Product Development: A Global View

Before plunging into a detailed description of the elements of fast product development, it is worth considering some background. In this chapter, we'll examine why fast new product development is so important, who the leaders will be, what companies are spending on research and development, and how it is that speed isn't the whole story.

THE NEW LEADERS

International and domestic competition is getting smarter and better every day. The new leaders will be those companies that consistently get to the market first with high-quality new products and that keep on introducing improvements to those new product lines. The new leaders will be those companies that learn to get greater value for each dollar spent on new product development.

There are plenty of American companies that have learned how to do fast product development:

AT&T worked hard to reduce product development time drastically yet lowering costs and improving quality. While it traditionally took AT&T more than two years to develop and market a new telephone, with improved development techniques, it took less than one year to develop and market its new Model 4200 cordlesstelephone.

W. H. Brady dramatically accelerated the pace of its product development cycle when it used a multifunctional team approach to develop and introduce its valve lock-out device in just three months.

Hewlett-Packard's new Laserjet printer was developed in half the time it would normally have required with older project management techniques.

Navistar learned how to develop a new U-Haul truck in half the time, fewer than 12 months from initial concept to full production. Navistar worked closely with customers and suppliers to shorten new product development cycle time.

The Japanese have also done well. In the last 20 years, they have taken over and dominated the worldwide consumer electronics business. This has been a humbling and ironic turn of events for American companies, particularly since the market had been based on American inventions.

The Japanese have been grabbing major market share in other markets as well: automobiles, cameras, small appliances, videocassette recorders, motor cycles and scooters, fax machines, and laptop computers. They are rapidly taking away market share in communications network switches, silicon wafers, memory chips, and computer displays. And they are becoming leaders in some of the newest technologies, such as X-ray lithography, optical storage devices, and flat panel displays.

These new leaders, as well as others, have mastered the concept that managing time is essential, that getting credible new products to the marketplace first will capture market share, and that with greater market share will come greater profits.

THE COST OF RESEARCH AND DEVELOPMENT

According to a recent *Business Week* survey,[1] American major industry spent about $70 billion for research and development (R&D) in 1990. This is more money spent on R&D than is in any other country in the world. Much of this money was spent on the development of new products and related processes.

In the United States, a lot of creative brain power is involved in R&D, more than 800,000 scientists and engineers. Japan has slightly more than 500,000 scientists and engineers committed to R&D.

The amount of money spent by the United States seems like an enormous amount, yet when it is expressed as a percentage of gross national product (GNP), the United States is actually lagging behind other countries. Japan is spending 2.8%, West Germany is spending 2.6%, and the United States is spending 1.8% of its GNP on R&D.[2]

The United States is lagging behind other countries in other ways as well. The Japanese have more than doubled the number of patents they have received for electronics technology since the mid-1970's and they license their patents more often than do companies in the United States. In 1990, the top three companies that were awarded U.S. patents were Japanese: Canon, Hitachi, and Toshiba. Only three U.S. companies were in the top ten: General Electric, U.S. Philips, and IBM.[3] In fact, of all the patents granted in the United States, 48% went to foreign nationals.

Companies tend to concentrate on how much they spend on R&D, amounts often expressed as a percentage of sales. This is an important ratio, but, while it is harder to measure, it is more important to consider the cost of lost opportunities. This is what a company loses in the long run if it doesn't do enough new product development or if it takes too long to get its products into the marketplace.

SHORTER WINDOWS OF OPPORTUNITY

In today's global marketplace, the window of opportunity for any new product idea is much shorter than it used to be. There was a time when a company could be fairly relaxed about the time it took to develop a new product. There was little fear about a competitor getting there first. Now, it definitely is possible to miss the window of opportunity just by getting to market a few months later than the competition.

DECREASING PRODUCT LIFE-CYCLE TIMES

The time between the introduction and the maturity of products has decreased drastically. In the electronics industry, for instance, average product life-cycle times have decreased from 3 to 4 years to 18 to 24 months. In the office furniture business, the typical office chair life cycle used to be 6 to 8 years. Now it is 2 to 3 years. This is true for many other industrial and consumer products as well.

Rapidly developing technology is one of the reasons why products have shorter life cycles. Technological advances make it more likely that innovative product improvements will be developed to meet an emerging marketplace need or create a new one. As a result, current products will become obsolete faster.

Further, news about a new product or new technological advance reaches the end user much sooner than it did earlier, and this results in an earlier switch away from an old product.

OTHER CONSIDERATIONS

There are other issues that need to be considered when thinking about new product development, such as

- Production runs are becoming shorter and shorter. A company can no longer count on maintaining a product in its original configuration for many years, milking it for profit without having to do very much to improve upon its design or function.

- The duration of exclusivity is decreasing as well. A new entry into the marketplace now enjoys a much shorter lead time before the competition catches on. The company that introduced the product can't take time to rest on its laurels. It has to move on to the next version of the new product or replace it with an entirely new one much sooner.

- Customers are now more demanding. There was a time when customers were satisfied with the status quo and they didn't realize that they had any rights. It's now widely accepted that customers have the ultimate power. Those companies that take a long time to respond to their customer's rapidly changing needs will find themselves bypassed by competitors who take customer's needs seriously.

WHAT HAS TO CHANGE

American industry has to get more and more credible new products to the marketplace, and it has to get them there faster. These new products must have high quality and functionality built in to them from the very beginning. There has to be increased partnering with customers and suppliers, and new products have to satisfy real marketplace needs. Just keeping up with the competition with "me too" products will no longer work in a global marketplace. American industrial leadership has to recognize that spending more money on new product development isn't the whole answer; rather, the money has to be spent a lot smarter.

The need to develop, manufacture, and market a rapid succession of products with relatively short life cycles creates a unique set of challenges for today's manufacturing companies. If a company intends to compete in the changing world marketplace, it will have to do its new product development extremely well.

THE VALUE OF SPEED

In today's cutthroat marketplace, speed, quality, profit margin, and price are essential ingredients for survival and growth. Of these, speed seems to be especially important. In fact, McKinsey & Co.[4] reported that going 50% over budget during the development of a project in order to get the product out on schedule reduces the product's lifetime profit by only 4%. However, staying on budget and getting to market six months late can reduce profits by 33%.

Offering a high quality product to your customers and satisfying their needs when they want to have them satisfied is what it's all about.

MANAGING TIME

Managing personal time to get more done in one day is only a small part of the story. Managing corporate time by speeding up the pace is what we need to focus on. It requires the acceptance of a philosophy that encompasses everything the company does, from product development to product shipping. It requires a full commitment from everyone.

Concentrating on speed requires an aggressive approach. It will be hard to achieve, and there will be plenty of inertia to overcome. There will be a natural tendency to resist change by people who are set in their ways. Companies need to accelerate the pace of everything they do, including the following:

New Product Development

By virtue of its capabilities as a fast developer of new products, Sony was able to establish its technology as the audio industry standard for the compact disk. It was able to beat out Philips, Telefunken, and Victor, all of whom had competing technologies for producing high-quality digital audio sound.

Sony introduced its first compact disk player in 1982 and, within four months, introduced four more versions at different prices in an effort to capture a greater share of the market. The strategy worked, and Sony became a world leader in compact disk player sales.

Today, the compact disk player market is substantial, and it may surpass the videocassette recorder in terms of consumer popularity. Sony has been able to hang on to its early lead in the marketplace because it got there first and because it was able to develop new follow-on products very quickly.

Response to Marketplace Needs

In the late 1970s, Honda's position as the world's leading manufacturer of motorcycles was challenged by Yamaha in what was to become a full-scale trade war that was known as the H-Y War.[5] Yamaha announced it was going to open a factory that, when it was in full production, would relegate Honda to the number two position in the marketplace.

Honda took up the challenge. It announced publicly that it would cut prices, spend more on advertising, and, most important, accelerate the pace of product modifications. It developed product modifications with a vengeance. Honda was able to introduce or replace 113 models by virtue of design and technology changes, turning over its entire product line twice during an 18-month period. During that same period, Yamaha was able to only develop 37 models. Because its models looked out of date when compared to Honda's motorcycles, Yamaha was unable to sell its motorcycles. Yamaha fell farther and farther behind and ultimately conceded defeat by stating publicly that the war had been lost to Honda.

The marketplace of the future will belong to those companies that get credible new products into the hands of their customers faster than anyone else.

Manufacturing and Shipping

There is no point to fast new product development if the new products can't be manufactured quickly. Fast product development has to be coupled to fast manufacturing if a company wants its new products to take off in the marketplace. Today's customers want their needs satisfied right away.

Stanley, a manufacturer of dining room, bedroom, and occasional furniture that ships directly to the retail trade, has set a goal of shipping to its customers within 30 days. This is opposed to an industry standard of 90 to 120 days. Stanley now has a competitive position in the marketplace because it satisfies the needs of its customers promptly. Stanley is growing at an annual rate that is nearly three times the industry average, largely because of its new shipping policy.

Response to Your Customer's Service Needs

Federal Express created a multibillion-dollar market niche when it discovered that customers would pay a premium to have their mail delivered overnight. Compressed time is an essential ingredient of the service provided by Federal Express to its customers. Until increasing competition and the fax machine emerged, Federal Express virtually monopolized the market.

Customers will pay a premium and will shift loyalty to the supplier that can satisfy their service needs quickly.

SPEED ISN'T THE WHOLE STORY

While speed is vital, companies should recognize that it is not enough to get a product to the marketplace first. The product must also satisfy a real marketplace need and meet customer expectations. It must be of high quality, it must perform well, and it must have an adequate profit margin.

To get the true benefit of fast product development, companies also have to have high-quality management and other talent, good channels of distribution to the marketplace, good advertising, good customer service capabilities, a good understanding of their marketplace and its needs, and enough money to do what needs to be done.

Companies also need to recognize that not all products have to be developed at the same pace. There are marketplace, technical, and financial considerations that should dictate whether a project is fast track or otherwise.

SPEED AS A STRATEGIC WEAPON

The companies that have learned that speed is a strategic weapon will excel in the marketplace. Companies that develop new products quickly and get these products out into the marketplace before anyone else will be at an advantage because they will have captured market share early.

You can be sure that your competition will be catching on to the fact that speed really matters. It's far better if you get there first.

Endnotes

[1]"The Brakes Go on in R&D," *Business Week,* July 1, 1991, pp. 24-26.
[2]"Report Warns of Decline of U.S. Electronics Industry," *The New York Times,* June 9, 1990.
[3]"Foreign Inventors Get 48% of U.S. Patents," *Research-Technology Management,* July/August 1991, p. 6.
[4]"A Smarter Way to Manufacture," *Business Week,* April 30, 1990, pp. 110-117.
[5]Stalk, G., Jr. and Hout, T. M. "Competing Against Time," *NY Free Press,* 1990, pp. 58-59.

2 Losing Big with Slow New Product Development

We are a great country with so many bright people. Yet we seem to have so much trouble moving beyond the slow, measured development of new products.

PHASED PRODUCT DEVELOPMENT

In the early 1970s, there was little doubt that N. V. Philips, the European manufacturer of consumer electronic products, would maintain its enormous lead over its competitors. But Philips actually lost its chance to develop a dominant position in the marketplace.

Philips launched the first practical videocassette recorder in 1972, three years before the Japanese entered the market. It took seven years for Philips to launch its next-generation product, the V2000, a VCR that offered longer playing time and produced better pictures. Unfortunately, Philips missed the window of opportunity because it used a slow approach to its new product development. During the seven years it took for Philips to develop the V2000, the Japanese had introduced three generations of VCRs. Philips was hurt badly by its slow new product development practices.

Many companies in the United States and Europe use a phased

approach to new product development, a way of developing products in an orderly series of steps, one step after another.

The phased product development process starts with a bright idea. If it appears that the idea is worth pursuing, it is sent to R&D to test its feasibility. If it is deemed feasible, it is then handed off to Engineering for design and prototyping. If it gets beyond that point, Manufacturing then is told about the project, and, more often than not, Manufacturing informs Engineering that it can't make the product or, if it can make it, that the product can't meet the cost objectives. At that point, the project goes back to Engineering for a revision of the design. Ultimately, Manufacturing gets a design it can work with, and it starts pilot production. Finally, the process ends with commercial production.

Whenever a phase is completed, senior management reviews the project to make sure it continues to meet its objectives. Often, the manufacturing people don't hear about the new product until they are presented with a set of final drawings. Marketing, Sales, Quality Assurance, Finance, Service, and Purchasing often don't get involved until some point near the end of the cycle.

Phased product development management is seductively pleasant. All the functional areas have their jobs to do, one after another, and senior management thinks everything is going well. In reality, phased product development is a disaster in disguise. It is killing us in the marketplace.

WHY PHASED PRODUCT DEVELOPMENT FAILS TO DELIVER

Phased product development creates products that are hard to make, that cost too much, that require too many expensive design changes, and that may or may not meet marketplace needs. It encourages isolation of functional areas and, worst of all, it's very slow.

It's slow because each functional unit has to finish its activities before the project can move along to the next stage and because communication is so poor.

Phased product development frequently results in poor product designs, and this can be a serious problem. No matter how good the manufacturing people are, there is no way they can compensate for poor design of a product. That's because most of a product's cost is already determined before the drawing ever reaches the manufacturing area. Overly complicated and poor designs cause severe delays in production.

Phased product development also takes a severe toll on people. It results in overworked and confused design and production people who are frustrated because schedules can't be met. It results in unhappy marketing and sales people who can't sell products that don't meet marketplace needs. It results in finger-pointing and the continuation of rigid lines between functional areas.

Slow product development results in late introduction of new products into the marketplace. A delay in introduction of only a few months can make the difference between success and failure in today's highly competitive environment.

A commitment to phased product development condemns a company to having to operate by crisis management, to always being in a reactive mode. The competition is often getting to the marketplace first with a new product or with line extensions that have new features. The company that operates with slow phased product development is struggling to keep up and is always having to deal with product problems that are the result of poor designs.

THE FUNCTIONAL BLACK HOLE

With phased product development, there is a failure of cooperation at the functional level. Projects enter the functional area whose turn it is to have the project, and the projects often are never seen again.

Even under the best of circumstances, there are functional turf issues and the various functions are reluctant to give up any authority. More important, they are reluctant to operate quickly. A phased approach to product development gives the functional areas a chance to exert the ultimate control over a project by never letting it see the light of day. They can take so long with it that, by the time the project moves into the next stage, it no longer matters. Many marketplace opportunities are lost this way.

Many American companies have allowed their functional departments to operate as independent kingdoms. This results in interdepartmental competitiveness and adversity. Communication always suffers when this happens. R&D, engineering, and manufacturing people are unable and unwilling to talk to each other. Marketing and sales people are often left out of the loop. Good new product development rarely occurs when there is poor communication.

MISSING THE MARKET OPPORTUNITY

A company that takes a long time to get its new products into the marketplace is more likely to miss the original opportunity. Markets and technologies change over time, and new products have to be delivered to customers while they still want and need them.

Slow product development increases the likelihood that new products will be irrelevant before they hit the marketplace. Slow product development makes it more likely that the competition will get there first with relevant products that capture market share.

Whereas slow product developers have to depend on major product breakthroughs to rescue them, fast developers can be fine-tuning their current products and making them even more responsive to customer needs.

Osborne Computer Corporation's first personal computer was popular, and it was not long after it introduced this first model that the competition started catching up. In an effort to retain market share, Osborne announced that it was about to release a new product with features that would be highly attractive to personal computer users. As a result, dealers stopped buying Osborne's old computers, deciding to wait for the arrival of the new model.

Unfortunately, Osborne's product development was slow and its competitors beat Osborne to the marketplace with computers that had the features Osborne had announced earlier. Osborne ultimately was forced to file bankruptcy and was no longer a player in a rapidly evolving market where fast new product development is essential.

American auto manufacturers continue to miss marketplace opportunities because of their slow new product development. It takes Honda and Toyota an average of two and a half years to develop a new model and introduce it into the marketplace; it takes U.S. automakers much longer, sometimes up to eight years. There is little wonder that Honda's and Toyota's cars are doing so well in the U.S. marketplace. By the time a U.S. car maker has completed one development cycle, Honda and Toyota will have introduced three models, each better than the one before it.

It took General Motors eight years to develop its Saturn model. By the time it arrived in the marketplace, Japanese cars already had many of the features that were touted as being unique to Saturn. The competitive advantage of being first in the marketplace with unique features was lost by Saturn.

IBM made a big deal about its new laptop computer and promised that it would be introducing it in the third quarter of 1990. Unfortunately, delays in development caused IBM to miss the introduction date. As a result, IBM could not be an early leader in a market that exceeds $3.5 billion in annual sales and is estimated to be growing at a rate of 24% per year.

HIGH COST OF DESIGN FLAWS

A phased approach makes it more likely that there will be design flaws. This is because manufacturing people will not have heard about the project until it is too late to do anything about any flaws that would have been obvious to them but not to anyone else.

Further, if design specifications are not frozen until late in the development cycle, flaws in the design may not be discovered until it is too late to correct them. If the flaw is serious enough, the project may have to be abandoned.

When a design flaw is discovered early, the cost of correcting it can be relatively minor. If discovered later, the cost can be astronomical. The electronics industry estimates that the cost of correcting a design flaw during the early design stage of a major electronics product might be about $1,000, while if the mistake is not discovered until the final production stage, the cost might reach $10 million.[1]

The reason for the high cost of correcting a fault in the design if it is discovered at a later stage is that, by the time the project has gotten that far, the company has committed to significant tooling and machinery costs. It's a profound experience if senior management is told that expensive tooling and machinery have to be scrapped because the development team did not discover a mistake until it was too late.

SETTING THE STAGE FOR FAILURE

The company that is likely to fail at its new product development programming will

- Use a phased approach to product development in which R&D, Engineering, Manufacturing, Marketing, and Sales hand the project off from one to another in an orderly series of steps.
- Develop products that have very little bearing on actual market-

place needs. Engineering and R&D people often are left out of the communications loop, and this helps assure that the needs of the marketplace will not be addressed.

- Have very little top management commitment to the development of new products, a management that says the right words but really is unwilling to let new product development teams exist or have any power.

- Be intolerant of risk and failure and have very reactive and defensive product development programs.

- Wait until its current product line is becoming obsolete or until the competition has taken a commanding lead before starting to develop new products. Failure to recognize that it takes time to develop credible new products often puts a company into a second best position from which it can never recover.

- Have top-down management where the senior managers do not listen to good people, where good new product development teams are not allowed to manage themselves, and where people are too busy putting out fires to take the time to develop new products.

- Ship new products before they are ready by minimizing or eliminating entirely the preproduction piloting and testing that is so necessary to debug the tooling and production process.

THE SOLUTION: FAST MULTIFUNCTIONAL PARALLEL PRODUCT DEVELOPMENT

American companies have to abandon their slow phased approach and start to develop a fast multifunctional parallel approach to new product development. This requires strategic planning for fast new product development and fast manufacturing start-up. It requires the use of multifunctional teams with all the key players in the development process on the team at the same time at the beginning of the project, and it requires a discipline that is applied at all levels of the company.

Endnote

[1]"A Smarter Way to Manufacture," *Business Week,* April 30, 1990, pp. 110-117.

3 Winning Big with Fast Parallel New Product Development

A company that has mastered the concept that fast new product development and fast manufacturing start-up is a sure way to achieve market share is Motorola, Inc. Motorola has become the world's largest supplier of wireless communication devices, such as portable telephones, pagers, and two-way radios.

Motorola's products account for more than a third of the world's $4.3 billion cellular telephone industry. It recently introduced the first cellular telephone weighing less than a pound and the first wristwatch beeper. It has licensed its technology worldwide. In fact, the Japanese government selected Motorola's technology over that of six Japanese and one European company as the nationwide standard for the next-generation cellular telephone. Motorola reached this enviable position by practicing fast parallel product development and by taking a long-term view of technology development.

Ingersoll-Rand used fast parallel new product development to develop its new air grinder in one year instead of the three and one half years it normally took to develop a new product. The project, called "Operation Lightning," used a multifunctional team to develop the grinder, and all of the team members were involved from the start. The team brought in a key supplier, Phillip's Plastics, at the beginning of the project to help select the material for the air grinder's housing.

At the beginning of the project, the team conducted focus groups in various parts of the country to learn what the customers and the distributors wanted. The team itself was responsible for design, and all its members were emotionally committed to the outcome of the project. Senior management was kept away from the project, although its members were kept informed. Even though the team had its occasional growing pains and headaches, the fast parallel product development process worked. Ingersoll-Rand learned that speed to the marketplace and quality and performance can go hand in hand.

THE ELEMENTS OF FAST PARALLEL PRODUCT DEVELOPMENT

Fast parallel product development is a process that is designed to get credible products into the marketplace as fast as possible by integrating design, manufacturing, and marketplace needs. It's not based on any one single element or magical formula; rather, it is a collection of principles that need to be practiced together. Successfully done, it's the best way for a manufacturing company to conduct its new product development projects.

The most important elements of fast parallel development are

1. Utilizing formal planning for fast product development
2. Engaging in front-end project planning
3. Using multifunctional terms for product development projects
4. Empowering the teams
5. Supporting the teams with adequate equipment
6. Gaining senior management support
7. Freezing product features and design specifications as early as possible
8. Utilizing components and processes already in existence
9. Eliminating most top-down go/no-go decisions
10. Ensuring continuity of team leadership
11. Minimizing the bureaucracy
12. Allocating time for the project
13. Assuring preproduction piloting

14. Co-locating team members
15. Seeding the next projects

Utilizing Formal Planning for Fast Product Development

New product development is too important to be left to chance. If you don't systematically plan for new product development, the results will never be those you want. The functional areas will never get the message that you are serious about a multifunctional team approach to product development, and they will revert to slow phased product development as soon as they can.

Engaging in Front-End Project Planning

The surest way to promote fast product development is to take enough time at the front end of the project to plan how the project will be done. This is the time to set objectives, to prepare the team, to identify key milestones and tasks, to establish senior management review points, to set up critical path project management, and to define and freeze product features and benefits. The time taken at the front end of a project by the development team will be more than repaid by faster cycle times, higher-quality products that have fewer design flaws, and more enthusiastic teams.

Using Multifunctional Teams for Major Product Development Projects

Multifunctional teams make fast parallel product development possible. The teams should be made up of people from all the key areas: R&D, Marketing, Sales, Manufacturing, Design, Engineering, Purchasing, Finance, Quality Assurance and anyone else who has something important to contribute. The team members should all be involved in the project from the start. Key suppliers and sometimes key customers should also be members of the development team. (See Chapter 11 for more details on team management.)

Empowering the Teams

A team without power is not really a team. It's just a collection of frustrated people who get together periodically. Teams need to be allowed to make critical decisions, and they need to have adequate resources and incentives. It's up to senior management to sponsor the teams and to give them the authority to make decisions and to draw upon company resources as they are needed. It's equally incumbent upon the team members to take the power once it has been offered to them.

Supporting the Teams with Adequate Equipment

Development teams need to have enough computers, software, test equipment, and anything else that might help speed up the process. Computer-aided design (CAD) and computer-aided engineering (CAE) systems speed up development by reducing the number of prototypes that must be built and by speeding up the overall design process. Stereolithography, a technique that produces intricately detailed, three-dimensional models, is another tool that greatly reduces the time it takes to make prototypes. The more complex the design process, the more time can be saved by using such equipment.

Gaining Senior Management Support

World-class new product development requires senior management leadership, involvement, and commitment. In companies that excel at new product development, senior management has taken a leadership position by developing objectives, goals, and strategies for new product development that are consistent with the company's strategic plan. These companies have a disciplined new product development program that is understood and accepted by all who are involved. Senior management makes sure that development teams receive full support and attention.

Freezing Product Features and Design Specifications as Early as Possible

Product features are a listing of what the new product has to do for the end user, a listing of form, function, and benefits. Design specifications are a description of how the product is to be made by the manufacturing plant and what it will be made of. Both features and specifications should be locked in as early in the development cycle as possible.

The problem, however, is that many projects fail or finish late because the new product's features and design specifications are not frozen early enough. The project end point remains a moving target, and the new product is likely to get to the marketplace late, if it gets there at all.

Engineers, marketing and sales people, and senior management often seem to have a lot of trouble accepting the fact that it's better to get to market first with a product that isn't perfect than it is to introduce a perfect product and miss the marketplace opportunity. They fail to realize that there is no reason why any follow-on improvements can't be used for line extensions, product modifications, and margin increases.

W. H. Brady Company, a manufacturer of industrial adhesives and identification devices, froze the design specifications of one of its new products early when it developed the "Tag- Out/Lock-On" device. The device, a plastic clamp that fits over valve handles, was developed in response to an Occupational Safety and Health Administration (OSHA) regulation that required manufacturers to make sure that valve handles could not be opened by mistake.

Brady's development team settled on product features and design specifications within several weeks and succeeded in developing and shipping the product to customers within three months. The development team saved any proposed changes to the design and used them to develop follow-on improvements to the product. The new product has been successful in the marketplace, to an extent far greater than the company thought possible at the beginning of the project.

Ideally, product features should be locked in within several weeks after a project starts, provided there has been adequate identification of customer needs. If prototype or soft tooling is planned, the design specifications should be frozen as soon as the prototypes have been made and adequacy of design has been demonstrated. Freezing of design specifications should always take place before hard tooling is ordered, even though a certain amount of tool debugging usually is necessary.

When it comes to freezing product features and design specifications early, company management has to be firm and realistic. It needs to recognize that follow-on improvements can be used for line extensions and margin increases. Yet, it has to be careful that design specifications are not frozen too early.

Utilizing Components and Processes Already in Existence

Wherever possible, it pays to use components that are already proven in mass production instead of having to design all the components of a new product from the ground up. Developing entirely new technologies, processes, and components adds precious time to a development project, time that could be better spent doing something else.

Eliminating Most Top-Down Go/No-Go Decisions

With phased product development, decisions on whether to proceed with the next stage are made by senior management, and this wastes a lot of time. A solution to this problem is to have the senior management meet with the development team at the beginning of the project and for all parties to negotiate and agree upon objectives, goals, costs, and critical milestones for the project. Senior management then empowers the team to make the go/no-go decisions at each milestone, provided the milestones are being met on schedule within the budget expected. Senior management needs to be kept informed of a project's progress on a regular basis and needs to get involved only when it is time to freeze product features and to authorize a major capital expense for tooling, machinery, or plant facilities.

Ensuring Continuity of Team Leadership

Nothing hurts a development project more than having changes in team leadership when a new milestone has been reached. In Detroit's auto industry, project managers change projects frequently, and this gets in the way of progress. For example, the design project for General Motors' midsized line—the Pontiac Grand Prix, the Chevy Lumina, the Olds Cutlass, and the Buick Regal—had three different project leaders over the project's lifetime.

When leaders are changed, the project is slowed down because each new leader has a learning curve to overcome. The team members have to get used to a new leader, and the new leader's biases have to be integrated into the project. Any momentum that the project had is bound to be lost, at least for a while. It's far better not to change leaders in midstream unless circumstances make it absolutely necessary.

Minimizing the Bureaucracy

A highly bureaucratic structure makes it very difficult for a new product development team to get started and to do its work on schedule. An important function of senior management is to examine the company's policies and procedures and to minimize the bureaucracy for the new product development team. While full documentation is an important function of a development project, the number of reports should be held to a minimum.

Allocating Time for the Project

Unless new product development team members have few other responsibilities, there will always be demands upon their time to do other things. This is particularly disruptive to a team that is attempting to finish a project as quickly as possible, especially when team members are on several teams simultaneously. The answer to this problem lies in careful setting of priorities, but care should be taken to not change project priorities frequently. Project teams can be very demotivated if they discover that their project has received a lower priority than it had before.

Assuring Preproduction Piloting

It is critical that there be adequate preproduction piloting of the product with actual production tooling and machinery before product launch. This allows time to debug the tooling, the machinery, and the process; to test production samples; and to train production workers.

All too often, marketing considerations cut into preproduction pilot time, and as many companies have discovered to their chagrin, this can severely compromise the quality of the finished product and yield inadequate profit margins. In a worst case scenario, preproduction piloting is skipped entirely and prototypes are shipped before actual production tooling is installed.

Co-Locating Team Members

How close the team members are to each other matters a great deal when conducting a new product development project. Close physical proximity of the team members goes a long way toward speeding up a development project because communication is enhanced. If co-location is not possible, especially if it's a large project, the team should be given its own meeting room where team members can gather informally and where it can post its critical path chart and leave other paperwork.

Seeding the Next Projects

Seeding the next new product development project team with a few key players from a team that has succeeded in its assignment is a useful way of shortening a team's learning curve. The experienced team members not only know how best to operate within a team, but they are also enthusiastic proponents of fast parallel new product development. They know the ropes, they know what needs to be done, and they are visible proof that success is possible.

INCREMENTAL IMPROVEMENTS VERSUS BIG HITS

In Western countries, it's the major projects that are most likely to get senior management's attention and support. Smaller projects rarely are viewed as being meaningful. Yet evidence is mounting that it is more profitable in the long run to continue to conduct development projects that deliver follow-on, improved products with more and more features than to try for one big new product hit.

A single large development project absorbs all the company's resources: money, manpower, energy, and enthusiasm. When a company focuses all its efforts on one large project, there are few resources left for the smaller projects that result in improvements in the current product line and increased market share.

Companies sometimes look to a single great product breakthrough to save them from a history of declining profits. They hope for a magnificent product introduction that will generate enormous revenues and result in a turnaround of the company's fortunes. At best, this is wishful thinking that will work only for the very lucky.

The fact is that the odds of success with *any* development project are not good in the first place. No matter the size of the project, only a few ideas for new products will end up as significant revenue generators in the marketplace. Since a minor development project has just as much chance of succeeding (or failing) as a large project, it pays to concentrate on the smaller projects. At least some of the projects will succeed, and, for any given amount of resources, you will be able to conduct a greater number of projects.

The downside to one big hit is *one big loss*. If all the development dollars are allocated to only a few large product ventures, odds are that substantial amounts of time and money will be lost in the long run.

The Baseball Analogy

The home run hitter receives all the applause and all the fame in baseball. He's the one who is most likely to be nominated to the baseball Hall of Fame. In America, we have a belief that home runs are much better than base hits, even though, in reality, a winning team has far more singles, doubles, and triples than home runs.

American business makes the same assumption, that home runs, in the form of major product introductions, are much better than incremental product improvements. Yet, as is the case with baseball, it is the company that succeeds in introducing a series of incremental improvements in its current product line with an occasional big hit that will deliver winning scores and championships in the long run.

The Concept of Incompleteness

A common feature of Japanese art is that something in the artwork is left slightly incomplete or partially undone.[1] The idea is that the viewer's imagination will fill in the blank with an image that will be even more pleasing to the eye than the complete image if it were to have been painted by the artist. Japanese manufacturers use the same concept when developing a new product. Management considers that a product is never finished. Employees are encouraged to think constantly of ways of improving the current product line so that it meets ever more needs in the marketplace. The net result is that incremental improvement is favored over major development projects, and new, improved products are moved into the marketplace faster.

Adopting a concept of incompleteness is a way of capturing greater market share. The development of the 35mm single-lens reflex camera is a good example of the Japanese concept of incompleteness. During the last ten years, Japanese companies have succeeded in breathing life into what had become a mature market.

In 1980, the big breakthrough was Nikon's point and shoot self-focusing camera. Other Japanese companies followed with a series of incremental improvements that assured Japan's domination of the market. Canon developed its completely automatic 35mm camera, and Minolta released its Maxxum 7000 automatic camera with specialized electronic systems. Canon, Nikon, and Pentax followed with cameras that featured many other new features.

This particular lesson from Japan suggests that we should view our products as never being complete and that we should send them into the marketplace in that condition, provided they meet high quality standards. We should plan on adding incremental improvements as quickly as possible. To the Japanese, incompleteness is not seen as a sign of weakness. It is viewed as an opportunity for follow-on features that will capture ever-increasing market share.

Mitsubishi's Heat Pump

Over a 13-year period, from 1976 through 1988, Mitsubishi introduced 13 incremental improvements of its 3-horsepower heat pump, enabling the company to gain a position of prominence in a very competitive worldwide market.[2]

During this time, Mitsubishi developed and introduced a different sheet metal configuration, remote control, integrated circuits augmented with microprocessors, quick-connect freon lines, rotary compressor, louvered fins, electronic cycle controls, an inverter for better speed control, shape memory alloys, optical sensor controls, hand-held remote personal controller, learning circuitry, and electronic air purifiers.

While none of the incremental changes involved major technological breakthroughs, each product improvement allowed Mitsubishi to pursue its strategic plan. The continuing flow of changes enabled Mitsubishi to gather and retain greater market share.

A Balanced Approach

From time to time companies will decide to pursue a major development project. This is fine, provided it does not limit the company's development activities to that project only. Because there is a risk of failure for any development project, it pays to find a proper balance of different-sized projects. Conducting small-, intermediate-, and large-sized projects simultaneously improves the odds for success substantially.

YOU DON'T HAVE TO BE A *FORTUNE 500* COMPANY TO DO FAST PRODUCT DEVELOPMENT

There might be a tendency to think that parallel product development with multifunctional teams is limited only to those companies that have large financial capabilities. Not so. The principles of parallel product development are applicable to companies of all sizes, even very small companies where there's very little cash and very few people to go around. In the long run, companies of all sizes are discovering that fast product development is less expensive in the long run because they are able to get relevant products to the marketplace faster and can hang onto or grab extra market share.

BENEFITS OF A MULTIFUNCTIONAL APPROACH TO PRODUCT DEVELOPMENT

With fast parallel product development, you can

- Reduce development time
- Require fewer engineering changes
- Improve communication
- Get to market faster
- Improve overall quality
- Increase productivity
- Improve the return on assets
- Command higher prices
- Increase market share
- Have more effective teamwork

    And, of course, you get a chance to keep playing the game.

MORE WINNING COMPANIES

By using a fast parallel new product development approach,

- Eaton cut the development time of a new tubular position sensor by 66%, completing the development project in just one year.

- AT&T cut its product development cycle time for its main phone switching computers in half, from three years to one and one half years and, in the process, greatly reduced its manufacturing defects.

- Hewlett-Packard developed its laser printer, the HP II, in half the time it had taken it for the development of earlier, less complicated printers.

- NCR cut the product development cycle time for checkout counter terminals to 22 months, a 50% improvement. The product had fewer parts, and its assembly time was cut dramatically.

- Deere cut its cycle time for construction and forestry equipment by 60% and saved 30% on development costs. It cut the development time for riding lawn mowers to just one year and learned the importance of having a key vendor on the team.

In every case, these companies practiced fast parallel product development, and they went on to capture significant market share within their product categories. They are maintaining their positions in the marketplace by continually rolling out follow-on products with new features and improvements and only occasionally coming out with a big hit.

THE PROBLEM WITH "CONCURRENT" OR "SIMULTANEOUS" ENGINEERING

"Concurrent" or "simultaneous" engineering are widely touted as a way of doing fast parallel product development. However, to say "concurrent" or "simultaneous" *engineering* implies that fast product development is strictly a function of the engineers. Not so. Fast product development is a process in which people from all the key functions, not just the engineers, are involved from the very beginning of a development project.

Endnotes

[1]Tatsuno, S. M., *Created in Japan: From Imitators to World Class Innovators* (New York: Harper & Row, 1990), pp. 122-123.

[2]Stalk, G., Jr. and Hout, T. M. *Competing Against Time,* New York, Free Press, 1990. pp. 111-114.

4 Starting a Development Project

TEN STEPS TO STARTING A DEVELOPMENT PROJECT

Once a development project has been selected, it's important that the development team be formed and start working right away. There are ten steps to be taken at the early stages of a project. They are:

1. Selecting the multifunctional team
2. Identifying the product champion
3. Selecting the team leader
4. Defining the mission and objectives of the project
5. Using critical path management
6. Estimating the project's cost
7. Seeking senior management approval to proceed
8. Establishing an accounting system to track project costs
9. Identifying customer needs early
10. Searching for the major concerns (the "troll" search)

Selecting the Multifunctional Team

There are two ways to approach team selection: either by assigning people to teams or by selecting volunteers from a list of qualified people. It's always better to have volunteers. Ideally, the first several team members are volunteers that are picked by management, and these volunteers select the rest of the team.

If the project is an exciting one, it will attract good people, especially if the environment is friendly to fast new product development and the project has senior management's support.

Core development teams should be small, consisting of no more than 6 to 12 people, all of whom have approximately the same rank within the company. Teams that are any larger seem to have a great deal of difficulty getting started, and they may achieve very little.

People who are on the team should be there because they really contribute something to the project and because they are totally committed to it, not just because they are a functional department's representative. Senior managers should not be on the team because the team will defer to them and everything will come to a halt when they are present.

If a key supplier is on the team, the selection of the supplier can be based on such considerations as ability to absorb additional business, adequacy of manpower resources, financial stability, quality programming, and an inclination to work as a member of a team. When manufacturing products that are for other equipment manufacturers (OEM) customers, it is equally important to have customer representatives on the project development team.

Identifying the Product Champion

If a new product is going to make it to the marketplace, it has to have a champion, a person who loves the project, who is high up in management, and who promotes the project throughout its critical stages. The champion is competent, knows the company, knows the market, has drive and aggressiveness, and is politically astute.

There needs to be a product champion for every major project, and the champion and the project leader should not be the same person. If no champion emerges, it might be better not to start the project because it may fail for lack of senior management support.

Selecting the Team Leader

The choice of team leader is critical. Without a good leader, the development project will go nowhere. The leader must have a forceful personality, an unwavering belief in the project and an ability to control a group of individuals without getting in their way. While team leaders are usually chosen by senior management, it is far better if the leader is selected by team consensus. If the team members believe the leader is their choice, they will be far more likely to participate fully and follow the leader's direction.

Defining the Mission and Objectives of the Project

This is an important first step for the new product development project. The mission for the project is roughly set forth by senior management and is finalized by the team. The project objectives are best originated by the team itself. The team needs to have a clear vision of where it is going, how it is going to get there, and when it will be finished. The project's objectives have to be realistic and achievable and very specific with regard to quantities, cost, quality, and completion dates.

Using Critical Path Management

The beginning of the project is also the time to define responsibilities and tasks and to make sure that computer-driven critical path project management is in place. The places in the project where approvals are necessary and where product features and design specifications are frozen must also be shown on the critical path, and there should be an understanding of who is responsible for the approvals.

Establishing the critical path is best done by the team itself, with the team leader taking responsibility for maintaining and distributing the critical path chart. (See Chapter 6 for more information on critical path project management.)

Estimating the Project's Cost

It's important that the team estimate the total project cost at an early stage of the project, as soon as the critical path chart has been completed. Costs include such items as direct and indirect labor, prototyping expenses, consultant fees, tooling costs, travel, supplies, and market introduction.

Seeking Senior Management Approval to Proceed

Once the project team is in place and the project's mission, objectives, milestones, time line, and cost estimate have been established by the team, it is appropriate for the team to seek approval to proceed with the project. The team should make a presentation to senior management at this time, keeping in mind that this should be a negotiative process.

Establishing an Accounting System to Track Project Costs

An accounting system to track project costs frequently is overlooked when setting up new product development projects. Many companies are totally unaware, except in the most general terms, of how much their development projects cost. Up-to-date cost information is essential if a project is to be well managed. This requires a special effort by the company's accounting department to set up a system to track and report the information in time for it to be of value to the team.

Identifying Customer Needs Early

New product features should be based on actual customer needs. The earlier these needs are identified by the product development team, the better. Simplified quality function deployment (QFD) focus groups and any other means to identify customer needs can be used.

Once customer needs have been identified, the product offering is then defined. This is a description of exactly what it is the team is intending to make, what are its features and benefits, and how it is to be positioned in the marketplace. It is based on an understanding of the customer needs and uses information obtained during the simplified QFD focus group(s) as well as other sources of information. (See Chapter 7 for more information on a simplified approach to quality function deployment.)

Searching for the Major Concerns (The "Troll" Search)

Soon after the team has launched the project, it is helpful if it takes some time to identify the team members' major concerns and, having done so, to take steps to head off those concerns. Here's how this is done:

1. The team meets with either the team leader or a facilitator who conducts the exercise.

2. The leader asks for major concerns by going around the table and asking each person in turn to describe one concern, starting with technical concerns and then moving into looking for manufacturing, marketing, sales, financial, quality, purchasing, and any other concerns.

3. Every person receives one turn in rotation, until everyone passes and there are no more concerns expressed. The concerns are written down by the leader as they are expressed on large sheets of newsprint which are then taped to the wall.

4. After all the concerns have been expressed, the leader asks the team to score each concerns likelihood and seriousness on a scale of 1 to 10 by consensus, where a 1 is a very-low-level concern and a 10 is a major concern. The scores for likelihood and seriousness for each concern are multiplied together and the resultant scores are rank ordered. The results of the exercise are then circulated to all the team members. A week later, the team meets and it considers all the major concerns, figuring out how each potential problem will be prevented.

This is a simplified Failure Mode and Effect Analysis and it is a powerful exercise for any development team. It should be repeated at each major stage of the development cycle.

OVERCOMING INERTIA

Inertia is the tendency of a body at rest to remain at rest, until it has a powerful enough force imposed upon it that moves it in a new direction. A company, like any other body, is unlikely to change its ways unless it is shaken up enough to make it consider changing its ways. It sometimes takes a cataclysmic realization for a company to decide to abandon its old, rigid ways and move into fast new product development. Outside forces drive the realizations that

• Your competition has come out with a new product that is resulting in the loss of major market share for your company.

• Your competition always gets to the marketplace first with better products.

• No matter what you do, you are continuing to develop products that are hard to manufacture, that do not meet marketplace needs, and that can't give you decent margins.

• Your key people are leaving to go to companies where the environment is more conducive to fast product development.

Even though there is a new awareness that something has to change for the better and that the change has to occur soon, it is still hard to overcome inertia. One good way to overcome inertia is to pick a project that has a high likelihood of success and complete it in less than nine months. This is the fast-start project.

An early success will go a long way toward overcoming inertia and it will be extremely gratifying for everyone involved.

THE FAST-START PROJECT

In a company that has not been practicing fast new product development, there will be plenty of nonbelievers who aren't willing to accept the parallel team approach. They believe that it just can't be done or that it can't be done in their company. These people have an emotional investment in keeping things the way they are. Their attitudes represent a significant amount of inertia that has to be overcome. They need to have proof that the concept is valid before they will be willing to give it their full support.

This is best accomplished by selecting some good people from a group of volunteers and by asking them to work as a multifunctional team on a small and relatively easy to accomplish new product development project. The intention is to get parallel new product development off to a fast start by developing a meaningful new product before the nonbelievers in the company succeed in sabotaging the project. A successful fast-start project builds momentum for other projects that are more complicated.

While the fast-start project is going on, senior management makes a big fuss about the importance of the project and gives it plenty of attention. The development team is provided with adequate resources, and nothing is allowed to get in its way.

At the beginning of the project, senior management works with the team to help establish the fast-start project's objectives, milestones, budget, and duration. After that has been accomplished to everyone's satisfaction, the senior people get out of the way and let the team do its work. The team is allowed to select its own leader, and it is encouraged to develop its own operating ground rules. The team uses computer-driven critical path project management. The team leader reports directly to a senior manager, ideally the chief executive officer (CEO).

There needs to be a champion for the fast-start project. This person should have a relatively high management position and should be someone who believes in the project and in the concept of fast multifunctional parallel new product development. The champion mentors the team and makes sure it gets all the support it needs.

While the team is doing its work, it and the project is given high visibility within the company. The project moves along as quickly as possible. When the project is finished, the CEO celebrates its success with companywide publicity and, as quickly as possible, forms other teams to start more projects. New teams can be seeded with people who were members of the fast-start project.

The choice of the fast-start new product development project is critical. It should

- Have a high likelihood of success
- Be important to the company
- Be compatible with the company's core technologies
- Fit within the company's marketplace niche
- Satisfy a specific customer need
- Be completed within nine months

The fast-start project is best selected by a team consisting of the CEO and a representative each from Marketing, Sales, R&D, Engineering, Finance, and Manufacturing.

MAINTAINING THE MOMENTUM

Overcoming inertia with one successful project, of course, is not enough. The momentum gained will not be maintained unless there is follow-through by the key managers within the company and unless there is a serious commitment to change. To do this, a number of steps have to be taken:

- Identifying more new product development projects and the start-up of more team efforts, making sure that project objectives are reasonable and attainable
- Ensuring the ongoing training of key management people in the practice of fast new product development
- Relocating or removing those people who insist on getting in the way
- Communicating continuously messages that promote fast product development
- Changing in performance expectations so that people within the company know that they are expected to move faster
- Improving communication and feedback to improve inter-functional relationships
- Shortening the learning curve by seeding people from successful development projects into other projects that are just getting started
- Simplifying the decision-making process within the company
- Making sure that everyone hears and understands the company's mission, objectives, goals, and strategies
- Modifying the infrastructure of the company to make it easier to accomplish team efforts and to minimize the bureaucracy
- Making certain that the right people are on the job

5 Considerations for Senior Management

SENIOR MANAGEMENT'S ROLE IN NEW PRODUCT DEVELOPMENT

Senior management plays an enormously important role in the new product development activities of a company. The chief executive officer has to

1. Set the stage by providing a vision and a plan for fast new product development
2. Make certain that the company's culture is supportive of fast product development
3. Make sure that multifunctional teams are used for product development and that the teams have the necessary resources

Some of the things that senior management can do to help promote fast and effective new product development include:

1. Developing and communicating the vision
2. Preaching the importance of speed
3. Identifying and overcoming barriers to fast product development
4. Finding the right people for fast product development

5. Staying informed
6. Empowering the teams
7. Emphasizing training
8. Minimizing bureaucracy
9. Seeking ideas
10. Identifying the marketplace needs
11. Establishing formal criteria for selecting projects
12. Prioritizing projects and matching the project load to available resources
13. Providing the resources
14. Making risk and failure acceptable
15. Insisting on quality
16. Being a cheerleader

Developing and Communicating the Vision

Senior management needs to oversee and guide the preparation of a strategic plan for the business in general and for new product development in particular, making certain that the plans are communicated to all levels of the company. Without a detailed understanding of where the company is headed and how it intends to get there, it's hard for people to know how to develop products that address the needs of the company and its customers.

Preaching the Importance of Speed

Senior management has to make sure that everyone in the company gets the message that getting new products to the marketplace quickly is essential for the company's well-being. The senior managers must prepare the message and continuously preach it, endlessly saying the same words and variations of the message until everyone buys in.

Identifying and Overcoming Barriers to Fast Product Development

There will be plenty of barriers when going down the path of fast new product development. These barriers include

- Poor middle management commitment

- Conflicts between functional areas
- Conflict within the development teams
- Not enough time to do the work
- Frequent changes in product features and design specifications
- Too many projects
- The "not invented here" syndrome
- Obsessive development

There will be times when concentrating on speed will cause disruptions in the operation of the company. Some people will sincerely doubt that fast parallel product development is a good idea. Senior management must be aware of the tensions that are introduced with change and take steps to deal with them. (See Chapter 8 for a comprehensive list of potential problems associated with product development.)

Finding the Right People for Fast Product Development

Senior management must find the right people for fast product development, either by growing them from within or by finding them on the outside. Because fast product development depends on the enthusiasm and capabilities of all levels of management, those who are unable or unwilling to make the change must be helped to understand that change is necessary.

Staying Informed

Senior management must at all times maintain an awareness of what is going on with new product development within the company. Without this awareness, management will not be in position to provide the necessary guidance and support for the development teams. The senior managers have to be able to hear about problems with specific projects without ever indicating a desire to shoot the messenger who bears bad news.

There is a delicate balance between keeping informed and getting in the way. Care must be taken by senior management not to meddle with projects once they have been started and to avoid making suggestions that are thoughtless or harmful. A suggestion made by a senior person carries far more weight than does a suggestion made by anyone else. If this person offers a suggestion, it had better be well thought out and not just a casual comment.

Empowering the Teams

Senior management needs to decide what kinds of decisions can be made by the development team itself. So long as it has not deviated from the original plan and so long as it is on track with regard to time and budget, the team should be allowed to proceed through the stages of the project without having to seek permission to go to the next stage whenever it has reached a milestone. Senior management should not have to get involved until it is time for the team to seek approval to purchase major tooling or some other capital item.

The teams should be allowed to purchase necessary equipment and materials without having to resort to purchasing procedures that delay their progress, to select their own team members, to decide when to travel, and to identify their own ground rules for operation. Without such empowerment, it will be very hard for teams to develop the necessary team spirit and speed of operation.

Emphasizing Training

Increasing the knowledge base of the company is a key role of senior management. Constantly improving capabilities at all levels of the company make it more likely that new product development will be a successful venture. A commitment to ongoing training will yield benefits in many ways: more and better ideas for new products, improved technological capabilities, better understanding of the marketplace, improved project team management and participation skills, and improved morale.

Minimizing Bureaucracy

Time and time again, development teams have trouble getting started because there are so many rules and regulations that have to be satisfied before anything can happen. Senior management needs to be sensitive to the fact that excessive bureaucracy runs counter to fast product development. Senior management needs to examine the amount of red tape in the company and simplify things for the development teams as much as possible.

Seeking Ideas

If there are no ideas, there will be no new products. Senior management needs to let people at all levels of the company know that their ideas are wanted and to set up procedures for handling the ideas when they come in.

Ideas must be positively acknowledged when they are submitted and publicly recognized when they actually become a project. Senior management should find a way to support half-baked ideas, to give them time to grow into a potentially valuable new product. Management should also make sure that there is a way to keep track of shelved ideas and to reexamine them periodically.

Identifying the Marketplace Needs

Many senior executives downplay their obligation to help identify marketplace needs, relying solely on their marketing people to do this. This can be a big mistake because the identification of marketplace needs, as a necessary prelude to the development of new products, is too important to leave to any one functional area or to chance. In this regard, senior managers can set an example by getting out into the marketplace, by talking to the customers, and by making sure that other key players within the company are doing the same.

Senior management must also make certain that all the available tools are used to identify marketplace needs, such as engaging in focus group discussions with customers and dealers, analyzing marketplace trends, identifying problems with current products, talking to suppliers, and collecting data from customer contacts. Above all, the senior managers must make certain that the company has a workable and complete marketing plan that is known and understood by everyone concerned.

Senior management must also make it a requirement that technical people spend time in the marketplace talking to customers. If technical people are isolated, they will be unable to contribute ideas that meet actual marketplace needs.

Establishing Formal Criteria for Selecting Projects

The criteria that will be used to select development projects must be clearly delineated and understood. If the criteria are not known or if they are unclear, it will be hard for people to come up with relevant ideas for new products.

Very often, the criteria for selecting projects are not well thought out in advance. Instead, the selection and prioritizing of projects is left to chance and intuition. It is up to senior management to make certain that the criteria that will be used to select projects have been established by a team consisting of people from Marketing, Sales, Finance, Manufacturing, R&D, and Engineering. It's important that the senior managers have participated in the process and that the criteria, once established, are formalized and widely distributed within the company. (See Chapter 9 for more details on establishing formal criteria for the selection of development projects.)

Prioritizing Projects and Matching the Project Load to Available Resources

Once criteria for selecting projects have been established, senior management should prioritize projects in order of strategic importance to the company. Having done so, senior management should make sure that the number and scope of projects does not exceed the resources that are available. Management needs to recognize that it is far better to do a few projects at a time very well than it is to do many projects at the same time with mediocre or poor results.

Providing the Resources

Without adequate resources, development teams will not succeed. Teams need to be provided with a number of resources:

- Adequate funding and manpower
- Training in team management, team participation, and critical path management
- Computers and software
- Computer-aided design equipment
- Laboratory equipment

- Materials
- A good place to work
- Access to information
- Easy access to management

Making Risk and Failure Acceptable

New product development is a risky business. A company whose senior management is risk averse and intolerant of failure will not be able to develop meaningful new products in a timely manner. There will be a certain level of anxiety within the company, and people will be so anxious about making mistakes that they will be unable to think creatively.

Senior management must work hard to dispel the fear of taking risks and the fear of failing. As is the case with everything else, actions speak louder than words.

Insisting on Quality

It's up to senior management to set quality standards for the company and to make it clear that high quality is the expected norm for everything that is done. In this vein, they must make certain that new product development teams consider product quality when they are developing design specifications for a new product. They need to do this at the earliest stages of the project to assure that the product meets the highest possible standards of quality.

Being a Cheerleader

Above all else, senior management has to be a cheerleader, a staunch supporter of fast new product development, a highly visible supporter of the development teams, a leader who keeps out of their team's way.

THE DANGERS OF A SHORT-TERM OUTLOOK

On July 13, 1990, the following article appeared in *The New York Times*:[1]

"Motorola has emerged as the world's biggest supplier of wireless communications devices. . .

"In some ways, Motorola does business like a Japanese company. For one thing, *it has spent heavily on research and development.* Such outlays totaled $784 million last year, or 8.14% of the company's $9.6 billion in sales [italics added]. . . .

"Much of the research spending goes to improve production rather than to develop new products. . . . Improved manufacturing helped Motorola cut costs last year and raise profit margins while expanding its share of the worldwide market for cellular telephone handsets to 32%."

On October 10, 1990, the following article appeared in *The Wall Street Journal*:[2]

"Although it didn't break out results, the Schaumburg, Ill. electronics company said the sector that includes cellular telephones had lower third-quarter operating results, *mainly because of heavy research and development expenses* [italics added]. . . .

"That news sent Motorola's shares tumbling in heavy trading $7, to $32.75. The decline clipped some $950 million from the company's total value. . . .

"Some Motorola watchers insisted the company is simply investing for the future—a strategy that has helped it move from an old-line television and radio maker in the 1950's and 1960's into a global leader in wireless communications. . . .

"Many companies would have been proud to mirror Motorola's latest results. It said earnings for the period rose nearly 15% to $102 million, or 78 cents a share."

What's going on here? Motorola is a company that obviously has taken a long-term strategic view of its new product development and process improvement. In the long run, that's good for the company and its shareholders. Yet, in the short run, it was punished in the financial marketplace for having done so. What does Motorola's experience tell us about the way American publicly held industry is forced by its shareholders to view new product development? Certainly, it gives the message that short-term profits are more important than long-term new product development, a necessary prerequisite to growth and survival. While adequate profits are essential to sustain a company, they are not an end unto themselves; rather, they are a means to grow the company for the future.

Taking a Short-Term View of Profits

"America thinks ahead 10 minutes, Japan 10 years." This is a quotation from Sony's Akio Morita and Japan's former Transport Minister Shintaro Ishihara, authors of *The Japan That Can Say No.*[3] Perhaps it's an unfair generalization because there are some American companies that are willing to forgo short-term profits for long-term growth. But, like most generalizations, it contains a kernel of truth that is worth examining.

A frequent reason for the failure of new product development in many companies is that their senior management has a short-term profit orientation. The moment it appears that quarterly or monthly profits or sales are down or flat, people are told to control costs. The next thing that happens is that discretionary programs are cut out, cut back, or not started.

Unfortunately, new product development programs, especially in their early stages, are thought of as discretionary programs, and they are the first to suffer. The net effect is that development teams are afraid to commit to a project because, down deep, they know that senior management is likely to eliminate or reduce the scope of the program when the going gets tough. People are less likely to submit their ideas for new products and fewer projects get started.

Meanwhile, the senior managers wonder why there isn't more new product development. With a short-term profit orientation, senior management is making certain that the company will not prosper in the long run. Companies that go down this path will have a cloudy future because they will have no new products or technologies upon which to base their future growth.

Cutting R&D and new product development expenses is an easy way to improve a company's immediate profit picture, but in the long run, it's extremely dangerous.

Taking a Long-Term View of New Product Development

The ultimate solution is that shareholders, board members, and senior management all must realize that new product development requires a long-term commitment and that new product development projects can't only be funded when the sales and profits are high. They must realize that intermittent or marginal funding of new product development is dangerous for the company's future well-being.

RECONFIGURING THE CULTURE FOR FAST PRODUCT DEVELOPMENT

Understanding the Culture

A company just can't drop everything and rush into fast parallel product development. The switch from phased to multifunctional parallel product development has to be done in an orderly fashion. If not, it's unlikely that the transition will succeed. The best place to start is with an examination of the company's culture.

A company's culture determines how its people view the company and what sort of permissions they have to do their job. The company culture has a lot to do with how quickly people are willing to adapt to the new message that multifunctional teamwork for fast new product development is the right thing to do.

There is little mystique to a company's culture. Even though they are not able to articulate the words clearly, everyone at the working level knows what it is. A company's culture is really a collection of messages, a few of which are overtly expressed and most of which are unspoken. Some messages are supportive of fast product development, some get in its way.

The kinds of messages that are communicated to people within a company that interfere with fast new product development are

- Don't take risks.
- Don't fail.
- Stay where you belong.
- Keep your ideas to yourself.
- You don't need to know what's going on.

- You can't be trusted.
- Don't appear to be different.
- Be serious.

The kinds of messages that are conducive to fast product development are

- It's OK to have ideas.
- You are valued as a person.
- It's safe to take risks.
- Take your time and do it right.
- Failure is tolerated.
- You are trusted.
- Your ideas are valuable.
- Working together is a good idea.
- It's OK to have fun.
- You are smart.

Everyone in the company is affected by the messages imparted by the company culture: senior and middle management, functional department staff, teams, support staff, and factory workers.

It's hard for senior management to change the culture. The difficulty is that, even though the company leadership may start saying the right words out loud, people tend to filter the spoken messages and convert them into the old ones. It's as if senior management and everyone else are speaking two different languages. People within a company have a vested interest in maintaining the status quo of the old culture, as if it were a safe and comfortable way of life.

Senior management has the most influence on the company culture and it is senior management that ultimately is responsible for changing it. Failure to take the company's culture into account and to take steps to modify it for the better will prevent a company from moving into fast new product development.

The Role of Middle Management

The middle management of a company is the key to shifting from slow to fast new product development. A senior management commitment is essential, and it must take place before anything else can happen, but it is the middle managers who have to get the message. Once they have become believers, they will act accordingly. Otherwise, they will sabotage the new programs, either intentionally or not.

ORGANIZING FOR FAST NEW PRODUCT DEVELOPMENT

Fast new product development is possible in all organizations if multi-functional teams are supported by senior management. However, some organizational structures tend to be more conducive to fast new product development than are others.

There are a number of options when considering how to organize a company for new product development. Among these options, the most common, but least effective, is the functional organizational structure. Less common, and more effective, are organizations based on product matrix or project matrix management structures or variations of these.

Functional Organization

With the functional organization, all the functional department managers report directly to the CEO. Typically, all new product development activities are located within one of the functional departments, such as Engineering, R&D, or Marketing. The project team leaders have little authority to cross over functional lines and team members are from only one functional area. As a result, new product development is rarely encouraged or successful because the functional managers often are more interested in furthering the goals of their departments than they are in cooperative efforts that might benefit someone else.

Product Matrix Organization

The product matrix organization also has functional managers reporting directly to the CEO. In addition, it has individual product managers who report to one of the functional managers, usually to the marketing manager. The product managers are responsible for new product development within their product lines. The organization is structured in such a way that the product managers have the authority to cross over and draw resources from all the functional lines to achieve their goals. This form of organization is more conducive to fast new product development than is the functional organization.

The major drawback to this type of organizational structure is that the product manager is responsible for managing old products as well as developing new ones. Because old products often require a fair amount of problem solving and putting out of day-to-day fires, there sometimes is little time left over for new product development.

Project Matrix Organization

In this case, individual major new product development project leaders report directly to the CEO, to a corporate executive who reports directly to the CEO, or, ideally, to a senior-level new product management committee. The project leaders usually are in charge of only one project at a time, and as a result, their efforts are not diluted. Because the project leaders have the full and visible support of senior management, they are able to draw upon resources from everywhere in the company. They rarely have to fear reprisals from a functional area manager who feels that his or her turf is being infringed upon. In this form of organization, new product development is most likely to flourish.

Ideally, the team leaders of major development projects would report directly to a new product management committee with regard to their team's activities and would seek approval from the committee for the expenditure of significant funds. The committee is made up of senior department heads from the various functions. Each team would meet with the committee at the beginning of its project to negotiate and seek approval of the project's mission, objectives, milestones, critical path timelines and budgets and, throughout the project's life, would keep the committee informed of its progress.

If the project leaders are required to report their project's progress to a functional department manager, fast new product development will continue to evade the company because the functional department's needs inevitably will come first, especially when there are critical problems to be solved.

RIDING THE "S" CURVE FOR PROFITS AND SURVIVAL

Defining the "S" Curve

The "S" curve, which measures incremental growth over a period of time, is generally used to describe the life cycle of a company. The curve represents the company's total sales revenues over time. An "S" curve can also be constructed for each individual product sold by the company.

At the early stages of product's life, growth is slow because it takes time to get ready for the marketplace and for customers to learn of its existence. During this stage, the curve is relatively flat or sloped gently upward. This is followed by a period of rapid growth during which the slope of the curve is steep. Still later, there is a slowing down period, and the slope of the curve again begins to flatten out. The period of rapid growth may take many years, although, with today's shortened product life cycles, it may be much shorter.

The Incremental Yield for a Given Amount of Effort

It takes more and more investment of effort and resources to yield less and less return as a product moves farther up its "S" curve. At the early stages of a product's life cycle, there is a large return in sales dollars for a relatively modest effort. Later, after all the easy things have been done, when the market is saturated and when there are already competing products, it takes much greater effort to achieve the same results. The only way to get back to a situation where there is a big yield from a modest effort is to create a new "S" curve.

Riding the "S" Curve

A company can take advantage of its positioning on the "S" curve, provided it knows at all times where it is on the curve. A successful company rides the "S" curve by doing nonstop product development and by continually introducing new products or line extensions into the marketplace. In this way, the company creates a never-ending series of "S" curves, one for each new product, and each curve builds on the one before it. The company never has to worry about entering a stage of senescence.

Timing is everything. The time to move on to a new "S" curve is soon after the current product enters the period of rapid growth in its life cycle. The time to move into new technologies is long before the current technologies have become obsolete. Unfortunately, many companies still operate by crisis management. They wait until they have a serious problem before doing anything to help themselves. By then, it is often too late. This is the case with new product development.

Companies wait until a product line begins to enter into the mature phase of its life cycle before they start planning for new replacement products or line extensions. They fail to take into account that it takes time to develop new products, that not all new product ventures succeed, and that each new product entry has a period in its own "S" curve where growth is extremely slow.

Technology and the "S" Curve

The technology within a company has its own "S" curve.[4] It's important for the technical leadership of a company to know where the company's technology is on the curve. As is the case with total sales revenues or revenues from individual products, the incremental return from a given amount of effort becomes less and less as the technology moves farther up its "S" curve. The easy technical problems have already been solved and what is left are relatively intractable problems.

There are signs that indicate when a technology is reaching a state of relative obsolescence. The warning flags should be out when relatively straightforward deadlines frequently are missed, when R&D and Engineering prefer to do process development work than new product development, and when the company's growth is coming from products that sell into narrower and narrower market niches.

Since technologies usually mature long before profits begin to slow, it is important to know when to move on to a new technology. It is equally important to know what that new technology should be. Jumping onto the wrong technology can be just as disastrous as staying with a technology that is becoming rapidly obsolete.

You can't wait too long before moving to a new "S" curve with your technologies. In 1970, NCR had to take a $137 million write-off when it waited too long to change from electromechanical to electronic switching equipment. By the time NCR was able to make the switch, it had lost major market share to Burroughs, which had recognized much earlier that electromechanical switching was becoming obsolete.

STRATEGIC PLANNING FOR NEW PRODUCT DEVELOPMENT

Most companies have a strategic plan for their business, yet few actively develop a formal plan for their new product development activities. They have a vision for their company's future path, but they omit one of its most important components.

You have to know where you are going with your new product development. A strategic plan is a necessary prelude to fast product development. It simulates the future on paper, and it is a way of controlling the destiny of your company. A strategic plan for new product development can be part of the company's strategic plan, or it can be a stand-alone document.

A good strategic plan for new product development enables a company to create proactive development programs that result in increased market share. A company with a strategic plan for new product development is more willing to take calculated risks and will have a higher than average success ratio for its projects.

The strategic plan for new product development identifies the role that new products will play in meeting the company's business objectives. It commits a company to a plan of attack for up to a 20-year period.

A strategic plan can contain a fair amount of detail. For example, Honda's strategic plan for its new product development called for it to combine technological capabilities with a deep understanding of the marketplace. Its plan states that technical people will spend up to two months each year in the field with customers. As a result, its technical people have a much better awareness of customer needs than do most other car makers.

Companies that have a good strategic plan for their new product development activities have a sense of direction and a dedication to the pursuit of new products. They know that fast new product development is too important to be left to chance.

A strategic plan for new product development

- Connects the company's business objectives to its new product development effort and provides overall direction for the product development process

- Identifies the role new products will play in the growth of the company
- Encourages aggressive idea generation at all levels of the company
- Provides a focus for idea generation and supplies the basis for formalizing the criteria that will be used for selecting development projects
- Describes the markets for which new products will be developed
- Provides guidelines for the measurement of the performance of new products once they are in the marketplace
- Motivates all the people involved in the planning process and helps communicate the message that the company is truly serious about fast new product development
- Provides an opportunity for people to contribute to the decision-making and planning process, giving them a feeling of participation and satisfaction

Endnotes

[1]"Beating Japan at Its Own Game: Motorola Is Leading in Wireless Devices," *The New York Times*, p. C1.

[2]"Motorola Profit Report Depresses Stock: Investors Counted on Cellular Line in Weathering Recession," *The Wall Street Journal*, p. A8.

[3]A. Morita and S. Ishihara, *The Japan That Can Say No*, (New York: Simon & Schuster, 1990).

[4]Wolff, M.F. "Picking the Right Technology Should be First Priority," *Research Technology Management*, July, 1981, pp. 5-6.

6 Critical Path Management of Development Projects

THE NEED FOR CRITICAL PATH PROJECT MANAGEMENT

No matter what its size might be, a new product development project is only a collection of tasks. When all the tasks are finished, the project is complete. How well the tasks are anticipated, how well resources are allocated, and how well the tasks are completed will determine how well the project is managed.

Project management is both a science and an art. If managed well, projects come in on schedule and within cost estimates. If managed poorly, a project will be completed late and over budget or, worse yet, never be completed at all.

A project leader needs all the help possible: senior management commitment, good team members, adequate funding, a good connection with the marketplace, well-defined product features, and adequate tools. Of all the management tools available to a project leader, those that assist in the planning and execution of the project have the greatest value. Critical path project management is such a tool.

CRITICAL PATH PROJECT MANAGEMENT

Considering the need for speedy completion of development projects, it's no longer appropriate to use pencil and paper techniques for planning and tracking a project's progress. Gone are the days when a project can be managed by instinct and prayer.

Critical path management can be used to determine realistic project completion dates and to define and schedule the tasks that make up the project. If knowledgeable team members use good critical path software from the beginning of a project, they will be less likely to be embarrassed by slipped schedules and late product introduction dates.

Critical path management also enables the team to determine what human resources are necessary to complete the project. This is important because human resources are usually the limiting factor in conducting a development project.

Good critical path software will enable the project team to answer questions such as

- How long will the overall project take?
- What are the critical tasks that must be completed?
- How long will each task take?
- When must each of the tasks be started and completed?
- Who will be responsible for each task?
- What resources will be required to complete each task?
- How will a delayed task affect the overall project?
- What is the overall cost of the project and the cost of each task?
- Is the project on schedule?
- How can slippage problems be corrected?
- How does the project's cost at any point in time compare to the budgeted amount?
- What is the most economical way to speed up the project?

Fortunately, there are a variety of computer software programs readily available to help manage development projects. Of these, the best suited to the purpose are those that provide critical path management in a graphic form that is easy to use and to understand.

CONTINGENCY PLANNING

In the management of any development project, the unexpected happens all the time. Not even the best team is able to predict everything that could possibly go wrong. Critical path management makes it much easier to deal with any contingency that may arise. It sometimes makes the difference between completing a project on time or not at all.

When a contingency arises, critical path management enables the team to examine its effect on the project. It makes it possible to reallocate or redirect resources to deal with the problem before it becomes even more serious and to minimize its effect on the project. With critical path management software, it is possible to play what-if games long before any contingency arises. This is a way of planning the best response to a major delay in the event that it occurs.

GUIDELINES

- Of the many ways of presenting a project time line, the simplest and easiest to understand by team members and management seems to be the Gantt chart, where project tasks, their times of completion, and their interrelationships are displayed graphically (see Figure 6.1).

- Critical path management is best started by the development team at the beginning of the project. The team should include all the key players involved in the project. If the people who have to perform the tasks are the ones who estimate the schedules, it is more likely that they will be accurate. After all, they have the most to lose by being wrong.

- The team should list all the key milestones and associated tasks it can think of at the beginning of the project. This will help avoid unpleasant surprises later on.

- A critical path diagram will be only as good as the quality of the information that is used to develop it. If there is poor identification of the individual tasks involved in the project or in estimating how long it will take to complete them, the critical path chart will be useless. Worse, it will give a false sense of comfort when, in reality, none is warranted.

- Product testing, freezing of product features and design specifications, preproduction piloting, management review and approval points should all be shown on the critical path chart.

- The critical path chart should be reviewed and updated regularly, whenever key milestones have been reached and whenever a major problem has appeared. A fresh copy of the chart should be distributed to everyone on the team. The updated version should always be compared to the original.

- Sophisticated critical path management should not be used for small projects. It would be overkill to impose critical path management on projects that are very small because it is apt to delay their completion.

- Provide training in the use of the critical path software to all members of the development team and to others who might be reviewing the chart.

- If the product features and design specifications are not frozen early, critical path management of the project is useless.

Critical path software should be versatile. It should be user friendly and should do time and cost calculations, displaying graphic scheduling for the project in an easy to read format. The schedule should show when each project task begins and ends, which tasks need the most attention, and how well costs are being controlled at any given point in time.

There are many different critical path management software packages available, and new ones are appearing all the time. They vary significantly with regard to ease of use, complexity, and type of graphic display. Ultimately, the best software is the package that the team is most comfortable using, the one it will be most likely to use. In the last analysis, using any critical path software is better than not using any at all.

Figure 6.1   Critical Path (Gannt) Chart
Manufacturing Company Product Development Project

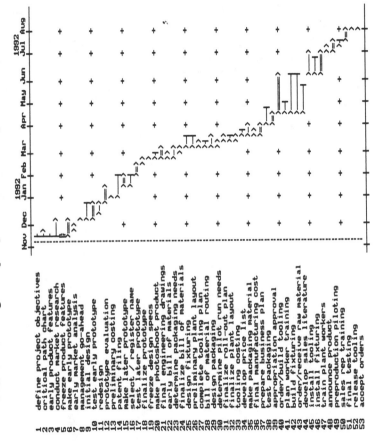

57

USING CRITICAL PATH MANAGEMENT FOR OVERALL PROJECT PLANNING AND RESOURCE ALLOCATION

Critical path software can be used to manage *all* the projects conducted by a department or a company. Here, all the projects are listed on the Gantt chart; each individual project is shown on one line with start and end dates indicated. Resources required for each project are estimated. This is a graphic way of analyzing project loading, comparing resources required with resources available.

When a department manager sees all of the projects displayed on one chart, it becomes much easier to prioritize projects and to know when department resources have been stretched too thin.

7 Building Product Quality into New Product Development Programming

It's hard to imagine anything worse than sending poor-quality new products to the marketplace. Once customers are disappointed, it's not likely that they will ever give you a second chance.

The Japanese weren't the only ones who have learned the hard way that new product quality must never be compromised. Toyota's and Honda's early versions of their Corollas and Civics didn't have very high quality in their early years. Customers stayed away from these cars until the manufacturers learned that quality had to be improved dramatically. Management everywhere is learning that truly successful product development builds quality into the product from the beginning of every project.

QUALITY MEANS CUSTOMER SATISFACTION

Building high quality into a product is not enough; the product must also provide customer satisfaction. When customers buy a product, they are doing so with the expectation that it will satisfy their needs and that it will continue to do so for a reasonable period of time.

In the last analysis, quality is not something that is done in the plant. Rather, it is an assessment by the customers of the product and the way it is delivered. Once having made that assessment, the customers render an opinion that is based on how well their needs were satisfied. It's that opinion that determines how much market share a product will gather. How the new product is designed and packaged, how it is delivered, how customer's complaints are handled, and how the employee-customer interface is managed all contribute to customer satisfaction. All these elements are important, and none can be ignored.

TOTAL QUALITY MANAGEMENT

The move to involve all levels of company personnel in the quest for quality is a good way of building a company culture that is conducive to the design and manufacturing of high-quality products. Total quality management (TQM) strives to improve the way the company is run and to improve the quality of its products.

Total quality management is a team approach that can help accelerate new product development. Anything, such as TQM training, that encourages multifunctional teamwork and teaches how to lead and participate in teams is a step in the right direction.

The philosophy of TQM conditions everybody in the company to think about high-quality performance in every aspect of his or her work. Introducing and embracing TQM programming is an important step along a path that ultimately leads to fast new product development and fast product manufacturing.

QUALITY FUNCTION DEPLOYMENT

Meaningful new product development depends on how well customer needs are taken into account and how well the new product succeeds in satisfying those needs. Quality function deployment (QFD), sometimes referred to as "the house of quality," is a method that is used to identify customer needs and to translate these needs into new product design specifications at a very early stage in the product development cycle.

Quality function deployment

- Helps produce products that will meet customer needs
- Speeds up the development process

- Prioritizes resources
- Focuses on customer requirements
- Reduces the number of design flaws
- Decreases the number of design changes
- Limits problems after introduction
- Promotes teamwork

Quality function deployment originated at the Kobe Shipyard a division of Mitsubishi Heavy Industries, Ltd., when Dr. Shigeru Mizuno helped in the development of "quality tables" in 1972. These quality tables were first used to plan new product development. Later, they became the basis of a technique (QFD) that was used to translate customer needs into design specifications.

Toyota was the first Japanese automobile company to use QFD by adopting the technique to develop its cars. It helped Toyota to produce cars that its customers liked, to reduce costs on new model start-ups, and to reduce new model development time. Ford Motor Company in the United States discovered QFD in mid-1983 and found that it significantly improved the design and marketability of its automobiles.

Quality function deployment stresses the views of the customers as opposed to the views of the engineers. When engineers decide what features ought to be incorporated into a product, customer's needs are not always taken into account. New products are made that may not meet a marketplace need, that may be wonderful from an engineering standpoint but do not sell, that are missing important features, and that fail to capture market share.

Basically, QFD starts when marketing, R&D, engineering, and manufacturing people go out and interview potential customers. The group attempts to determine what the customers would want a new product to do and what features it ought to have. A detailed listing of customer needs is developed, and this list is used to guide the product development process. The customer's needs are placed in logical groups, and corresponding design specifications (counterpoint characteristics) are described and developed to match the expressed needs. The product features are frozen as early as possible.

With QFD, it is easy to relate a customer need to a particular aspect of the design and just as easy to eliminate all superfluous aspects of the design that do not actually meet a need. It's much easier to understand the complex interrelationships between customer needs and design specifications.

A SIMPLIFIED APPROACH TO QUALITY FUNCTION DEPLOYMENT

When using QFD, however, it doesn't pay to get too complicated. For the most part, it's not necessary to construct the whole "house of quality" and to go through all the steps of the formal QFD process. What matters most is that multifunctional teams visit with the customers to discover their needs and that these needs are related to product features and design specifications. With this simplified scenario, the following happens:

- Customers are identified and invited to a meeting.

- The development team prepares and prioritizes a list of issues it would like addressed by the customers.

- Customers and four or five team members meet together in a room with a facilitator.

- For the first 20 to 30 minutes, the facilitator explores customer needs and wants, using the list of issues as a guide. During this time, the team just listens.

- Answers to questions and identified customer needs are recorded on sheets of newsprint. The sheets are taped on a wall in the room.

- For the balance of the 2-hour session, the team members get actively involved in the discussions with the customers. Customer wants and needs are consistently sought out, and team members try out their ideas on the customers.

- Toward the end of the session, the facilitator asks the customers to rank each identified need and proposed product feature on a scale of 1 to 10, where 10 is a need or feature that is considered to be essential. The rankings are recorded on the sheets of newsprint alongside each identified need.

- Later, the customer needs are recorded according to rank order and the list of needs is circulated to each team member. A special team meeting is scheduled later to discuss the findings of the session.

- It helps if customers can be shown a rough model or a rendering of the new product being considered or a sample of the old product being replaced.
- The session is scheduled so that team members and customers can have a meal together afterward. This allows for more discussion and further opportunity for team members to identify other customer needs.

The selection of customers is important and it is not always clear who the customers are. In most cases, it is obvious: the customer is the end user of the product. In other cases, the customer is less obvious. Here, the customers might be product specifiers such as architects, installers, tradespeople, space planners, or product distributors.

The benefits to a simplified approach to quality function deployment are the following:

- It yields results quickly.
- It makes it more likely that the new product will satisfy customer needs.
- It promotes the thinking process, and it quickly identifies ideas that won't sell.
- It is a simple, easy to understand approach (unlike classical QFD).
- It fosters teamwork.

HAVING A QUALITY ASSURANCE PERSON ON THE TEAM

To do fast and high-quality new product development, it's essential that an experienced quality assurance person be on the new product development team from the beginning of the project. All too often, a quality assurance person is not brought into the development project until the new product is just about to be manufactured. By that time, it is much too late for that person's input to have any real value.

Failure to include a quality assurance person on the team from the very beginning of the project can result in new products that are less robust, that are more susceptible to variations in materials and processes, and that may require extensive sorting to cull out the defects. It also can result in manufacturing yields that are unacceptably low and products that have poor gross margins.

FASTER NEW PRODUCT DEVELOPMENT MEANS HIGHER-QUALITY PRODUCTS

The statement "Haste makes waste" is widely ingrained in our culture. There is a belief that when development is faster, it is more likely that it will develop poorer-quality products. In reality, the opposite is true. The shorter the new product development cycle, particularly if the project is conducted by a multifunctional team, the fewer opportunities there are to make mistakes that will cause quality problems later on. Concentration on speed forces a development team to focus on those elements of a product's design that are most related to quality.

Based on a study by the National Institute of Standards and Technology, overall quality improves as much as 200 to 600% with fast multifunctional parallel product development.[1] When Ford involved suppliers in its fast product development teams, its overall product quality improved 60%. When AT&T shortened the development cycle time of its main telephone switching computers from three years to one and one half years, its manufacturing defects dropped 87%.

Endnote

[1] "A Smarter Way to Manufacture," *Business Week*, April 30, 1990, pp. 110-117.

Barriers to Fast New Product Development: Some Potential 8 Problems

It's unrealistic to think that there won't be plenty of problems when a company tries to move into fast new product development. Many of these problems need to be addressed before trying to start major projects. Others will appear after projects start and will have to be dealt with as they emerge. Some of these potential problems are

1. Lack of senior management commitment
2. Old messages
3. Failure to communicate strategic objectives and goals
4. Failure to have a formal development program
5. Rigid structure
6. Unwilling champions
7. Unrealistic expectations by management
8. Functional area willingness to cooperate
9. Lack of middle management support
10. Informal criteria for evaluating potential projects

11. Too many projects
12. Unwillingness to take risks or tolerate failure
13. Poor idea generation
14. Failure to address marketplace needs
15. Lack of a clear vision of the project
16. Conflict within the team
17. Bad experiences with teams
18. Frequent changes in team leaders
19. Inadequate technological base
20. Frequent changes in product features and design specifications
21. Obsessive development
22. Team members not co-located
23. Inability to visualize the product
24. Not enough time to do the work
25. Not enough money
26. Releasing a new product before it's ready
27. Budget overruns
28. Running out of time
29. The "not invented here" syndrome
30. Using multifunctional teams for every project

Lack of Senior Management Commitment

Senior management can fail to be supportive of fast new product development by not believing that new products are necessary for the company, by not believing that speed is of the essence, by not believing that their people are capable of fast product development, or by not believing that multifunctional teams are the best way to develop new products. Senior management may not truly be committed to the idea that introducing a steady flow of meaningful new products to the marketplace is essential for the long-term growth and survival of the company.

A senior management that says the right words but, in reality, is committed to the status quo is the most serious barrier of all. People who are trying to initiate fast new product development will be frustrated, and everything will grind to a halt or not get started in the first place.

Old Messages

In any company that has been around for a while, it is inevitable that people will be thinking (and often saying) messages that inhibit effective new product development, such as

"We never did it that way before."

"We tried the team approach once and it didn't work."

"We've got enough products in the marketplace already. Why do we need more?"

"We're much too busy to tackle anything else."

"If it ain't broke, don't fix it."

These are powerful messages, and it takes a continuing effort to overcome them. New messages have to be stated and restated until people begin to understand that the company leadership is serious about getting new products to the marketplace faster. Even then, they may still be reluctant to change.

Failure to Communicate Strategic Objectives and Goals

Many companies do not have well-thought-out objectives and goals. Other companies have well developed statements about their objectives and goals, but they do not communicate them to people at all levels of the organization. Yet these same companies expect people to come up with ideas for new products that will help further the aims of the company. If people have a poor or nonexistent understanding of the company's strategic objectives and goals, it's doubtful that they will be able to respond in a meaningful way to the company's needs for growth and change.

Failure to Have a Formal Development Program

Fast new product development is too important to be left to chance, yet that is just what happens when there is not a strategic plan for new product development. A good strategic plan makes it possible to create a set of companywide formal guidelines for fast new product development that can be used to guide the process through all its stages.

Rigid Structure

Some companies have so many deeply entrenched departments and functional lines of authority that there is little chance of change. Because of the way they are structured, they can't shift to a multifunctional parallel approach to new product development or even consider doing anything quickly.

People within a company can be very unwilling to abandon their old habits. If they persist in their old habits, the net result is that a switch to fast new product development is not very likely to occur. Such companies will continue to use a phased hand-off approach to new product development. Products will get to the marketplace late, if at all; they will fail to meet customer needs; they will be hard to manufacture; and they won't meet cost expectations.

People sometimes are afraid of a multifunctional team approach, especially if they are told they have to do things a lot faster. They experience a structure loss as they give up the old, comfortable isolation of their functional area, and that is frightening to them.

Unwilling Champions

The appearance of a product champion is essential for the well-being of a major development project. Ideas for new products can wither in the absence of a champion. The champion's role is to encourage the project during its critical stages by maintaining an awareness of the project's status, by mentoring the team leader, by helping the team get its needs met, and by enthusiastically promoting the product at the highest levels of the company. Product champions have to be true believers in the product and in the development team. If they are not, they are champions in name only. Ideally, champions are not chosen by management. Rather, they emerge from the senior management level of the company. For whatever reason, they have gotten excited about the product.

Unrealistic Expectations by Management

While it is appropriate to continue to strive for fast new product development, it is possible to lean too far in that direction. A management that imposes unrealistically tight time deadlines for development projects in its eagerness to get products into the marketplace is likely to find that the development teams miss nearly all the milestones. This is more likely to occur when the project teams have little or no say in the timing of the projects.

Functional Area Unwillingness to Cooperate

Functional areas within a company are apt to be managed as if they were independent fiefdoms. They sometimes are unwilling to cooperate with each other. This gets in the way of fast new product development, which depends on the ability of people from each functional area to work together on a team where each person can be counted on to do his or her fair share.

In a company that is organized along strictly functional lines, there is often very little cooperation among the functions unless it is mandated by senior management. Ordinarily, the functional manager's role is to promote the best interests of his or her department. Anything else, such as new product development, interferes with the operation of the department. Protection of the turf becomes the order of the day, and every functional area acts as if it doesn't need anyone else.

Especially with companies that have been around for a while, the functional departments have had a long time to get comfortable with the old arrangement. They have virtual autonomy, plenty of power, and the ability to sabotage a development program they don't like. When the company leader tries to convince them that a fast multifunctional team approach is best for product development, there is likely to be a lot of resistance, even though it won't be expressed overtly.

With a phased approach to product development, when it is the functional department's turn to tackle a new product development project, the project seems to drop into a black hole from which it never emerges. The functional department is extremely busy managing its day-to-day activities in support of the income producing activities of the business. The new product development project gets lost in the paper shuffle, never to be seen again.

Lack of Middle Management Support

In the final analysis, it's a company's middle management that is responsible for making things happen. Middle managers must be completely behind a program for it to work. Thus, even though senior management may be totally committed to the concept of fast parallel new product development, such an approach will never succeed if middle management remains unconvinced of its validity. While they might say the right words, their passivity or overt hostility will sabotage any development projects that are started.

Informal Criteria for Evaluating Potential Projects

Ideally, ideas for new products should be evaluated by the same set of formalized criteria, even if different people review the proposed projects. People should know what these criteria are. If the same criteria are not used uniformly and fairly, people who submit ideas will be confused about what the company really wants and the idea flow ultimately will dry up.

Unless a company has well-developed written criteria for evaluating ideas for potential new projects in place, it is unlikely that its people will recognize good opportunities for new products when they appear.

Too Many Projects

It's not unusual for a company to have far too many projects for the manpower resources available. The net result is that people are frustrated, anxious, and overloaded, and they can't seem to get anything finished on time. Senior managers are equally frustrated, and they are prone to making disparaging remarks about the development teams.

One problem is that projects aren't prioritized very well, and it is all too easy to keep on adding projects to the list of active projects. Another problem is that it's hard for companies to kill development projects, even those that seem to be going nowhere.

Unwillingness to Take Risks or Tolerate Failure

The people who are responsible for new product development are smart. They know that new product development is a risky business.

If the company's culture is not supportive of risk and tolerant of failure, development people will be more conservative in their approach to designing products or solving problems. In such an environment, dull or mediocre new products will be developed. An unwillingness to take risks can occur at all levels of the company. Since new product development, by its very nature, is a risky proposition, this attitude imposes a severe barrier to successful product development. If you look into the history of most companies, you will find instances where people have been punished for having made a mistake. While this may have been a rare occurrence, people tend to remember such events, and they are reluctant to take risks.

Poor Idea Generation

The development of credible new products is based on a steady flow of ideas, ideas for new products and ideas about how to develop them. If there is poor idea generation, either because there is no means of tapping into people's creativity or because people don't want to come forth with their ideas, meaningful and fast new product development will be handicapped.

In some companies, people are reluctant to submit their ideas. This will happen if people believe that management will not listen, if there is little chance that anything will come of their ideas, or if there are inadequate rewards for ideas that become commercially successful products.

Failure to Address Marketplace Needs

The whole idea behind product development is to design products that meet a well-defined marketplace need. Sometimes the marketplace need is obvious, and simply modifying a currently existing product is all that it takes to satisfy that particular need. Most of the time, it's not that simple.

If the company doesn't make a significant effort to uncover marketplace needs with adequate market research, it won't be able to develop meaningful new products. Talking to key customers, identifying market trends, using classical or simplified quality function deployment at the beginning of a project, conducting focus groups, tracking customer problems, conducting a market gap analysis, and learning from suppliers and competitors are all means of identifying marketplace needs.

Lack of a Clear Vision of the Project

A development project has to have a vision, a set of objectives and goals that is clearly set forth at the beginning of the project. Everyone on the team has to take part in establishing the vision, and senior management has to approve of the vision. If the team does not have a well articulated vision of the project, it will not be able to identify key progress milestones, and it will not know when it is finished with the project. Products developed without a clear vision will be late in getting to the marketplace, may be difficult to manufacture, and may not even meet customer needs.

Conflict Within the Team

Some degree of conflict is inevitable and healthy. Too much can be a disaster. The fact is that not all people are capable of working well with others, and, for whatever reason, they cause conflict within the team. Teams that are in conflict will lose sight of their objectives, concentrating instead on their dissension instead of the task at hand. The team leader must watch out for conflict and deal with it as it emerges because, without harmony, teams will not function well.

Bad Experiences With Teams

In the early days of the organization of quality circles, there was a great rush to form teams for the express purpose of solving quality and production problems. Unfortunately, the teams were not always managed well, and team member expectations were not realized. In some cases, employee bitterness resulted, and people were disenchanted with the idea of using teams for anything. In such a setting, the use of multifunctional teams for fast new product development will not be viewed with great favor.

Frequent Changes in Team Leaders

A development team always suffers from changes in team leadership.

Each new leader, especially if the person is not selected by the team from within its ranks, has a learning curve that has to be overcome. It takes time for team members to get used to a new leader. When there is a new leader, all forward movement can come to a halt, until team members become comfortable with their new leader and vice versa.

Inadequate Technological Base

New product development requires some degree of technological proficiency. If there's not an adequate technical base within the company, it may become necessary to go outside to acquire it. It may be too late to matter by the time this is accomplished. The marketplace need may have disappeared, or a more technically proficient competitor may have gotten there first.

Frequent Changes in Product Features and Design Specifications

If product features and design specifications are not frozen as soon as possible in the development process, the team will be frustrated and will have difficulty completing its task. There must be a commitment to the concept that product features and design specifications have to be frozen as early as possible and not be changed except under very unusual circumstances.

In fact, there are only three interdependent variables to consider when doing product development: time, product features, and quality. As is usually the case, management is unwilling to sacrifice quality or to agree to a later project completion date. In many cases, a project's completion date is predetermined by market considerations and it cannot be changed. Given these circumstances, if the product features are not frozen, quality inevitably will suffer because there will not be enough time to do adequate preproduction piloting and testing. (By the way, this consideration is a strong argument for freezing product features early and keeping them frozen.)

Obsessive Development

It is contrary to human nature to be satisfied totally with a design of a new product. People strive for perfection, but the reality is that, as far as products are concerned, perfection in design rarely is unattainable. People think of new products, customer needs keep changing, and new materials are constantly emerging. What was today's best design may turn out to be wholly inadequate in the future. This means that there is little point in trying to attain perfection in the design of the first market entry of a new product at the expense of getting the product to the market late.

Design engineers and marketing and sales people know that they can always find improvements and features that, when added to a design, would make it function better or give it a better appearance. In their obsessive quest for perfection, they keep on modifying the design, but they fail to realize that time is passing.

Past a certain point, more improvements and features add little to the value of a product as it is perceived by the customer. If a product meets a customer need to begin with and is of good quality, a basic design is all it takes to establish a position in the marketplace. Customers will buy from the company that is first to satisfy their needs with a credible new product.

"Obsessive development" is particularly frustrating to the members of a development team because they never know when they are finished with a project, they consistently miss deadlines, and the project costs far more than anticipated. Worst of all, it results in products that arrive too late in the marketplace to benefit the company.

Team Members not Co-Located

It's hard for a multifunctional development team to operate smoothly if its members are separated by significant distances. There needs to be face-to-face contact if relationships are to develop. When team members are separated from each other, they are unable to brainstorm ideas, they are more likely to lose interest, they may not devote the time necessary to do the work, they are more prey to functional turf issues, and they tend to lose sight of the project's objectives. The problem becomes particularly acute when the team members are located in different buildings or different states.

In the early 1970s, Monsanto's Biodize Division had its researchers in Dayton, Ohio, and St. Louis, Missouri; its engineers scattered widely at field locations around the country; and its marketing staff and a small testing laboratory on Long Island, New York. There was little effective communication among these key players. Development projects were rarely completed on time, they missed cost targets, and they rarely met the customer's needs the first time around.

The Monsanto Biodize experience is by no means unusual. There are instances where product designers and manufacturing facilities are in different countries. Under these circumstances, it is very difficult for technical and marketing people to communicate effectively.

The problem of physical separation can be severe when companies use outside contract engineers and designers and outside manufacturers and assemblers. The best way to overcome the difficulties in communication imposed by such a situation is to bring these people into the product development team at the beginning of the project, to give them a chance to voice their opinions, and to encourage them to make helpful suggestions. Sometimes, video conferences can help. When Apple Computer did a joint effort with Sony to develop a new laptop computer, it was able to overcome the communication problem with video telephone conferencing.

Inability to Visualize the Product

Marketing people and others often are unable to visualize what the final product will look like after the development is completed. Yet they are forced to make early design decisions based on two-dimensional line drawings that were presented to them by the engineers.

The engineers have little difficulty in looking at a line drawing and imagining what the final, three-dimensional product will look like. Others, whose brains don't function that way, are unable to make the mental leap. What often happens is that the marketing people look at the final prototype and realize that it has no bearing on what they thought they had approved earlier. They then insist on changes in the design, and a great deal of time is wasted in making new prototypes.

Most people need to see something that represents a three-dimensional view or to be able to touch and hold a model before they can be comfortable with their decisions to go ahead with a product. A way to do this is to ask the engineers to make artistic sketches or renditions of their proposals that are easier to visualize. Another way is to lease or invest in stereolithography equipment that quickly can produce detailed three-dimensional models from engineering drawings or to use three-dimensional computer imaging software.

Not Enough Time to Do the Work

Most often, team members are required to do many things other than new product development and their product development projects suffer. It's hard for a team member to resist a call to put out a fire or to solve a manufacturing problem that has suddenly appeared. Ironically, while they may be doing an excellent job of putting out fires, they are missing the point entirely, that without new product development there will be a bleak future for the company.

Frequently, team members are assigned to be on more than one development team at a time. There's nothing wrong with this, provided they can juggle time well and do the work required by the projects. This becomes problematic when people are on too many teams or if they have so many other assignments that they are unable to get anything done well. Under these circumstances, it is possible to burn out even the best people.

Not Enough Money

It takes an uninterrupted flow of money to undertake successful new product development. A development team needs to know that it will be able to complete its tasks without having to worry about the funds drying up. New product development will be successful only if promised funds are available at all times, not just when things are going well for the company.

Releasing a New Product Before It's Ready

It's not a good idea to send newly developed products into the marketplace before manufacturing processes have been fully worked out, before final tooling has been installed and debugged, and before all the marketing and sales programs have been implemented. If released before they are ready, even if tooling isn't involved, products are likely to have quality problems once they hit the marketplace.

The following scenario sometimes occurs:

1. Announce the new product to the marketplace at a national or regional trade show or sales meeting before the development has been started. Make sure the customers and salespeople get excited about the new product and that they eagerly await its appearance.

2. Complete the design and develop the product but only commit to soft tooling. This is cheaper, but it limits the design possibilities and develops products with a higher likelihood of having defects.

3. Release the product in nationwide distribution before completing preproduction piloting and before the product is ready.

4. Experience product quality and functionality problems and pull the product from the marketplace.

5. Take six months or more to fix the problems while, at the same time, attempt to placate disgruntled salespeople and frustrated customers.

6. Reintroduce the product and attempt to reestablish a position in the marketplace. Repeat as often as is necessary.

7. Finally, when sales seem assured, commit to hard tooling.

This is an approach that rarely helps the company. It can leave salespeople and customers with a very bad feeling.

A variation of this approach can occur when prototypes are shipped as if they were finished products. Market pressures sometimes force this situation and it rarely is a safe thing to do.

Budget Overruns

It's not unusual for development projects to exceed budget because it's hard to anticipate all possible contingencies. Yet development projects are sometimes dropped because they turn out to be more expensive than originally estimated, or, if continued, they are reduced in scope.

It would be better if development teams learned to do better cost estimates in the first place. Using computer-driven critical path charting to identify all the tasks that contribute to the development program helps avoid the problem of budget overruns by making it easier to plan needed resources.

Running Out of Time

Sometimes development projects literally run out of time. They have taken so long to be completed that either the marketplace need has disappeared or the competition has gotten there first. In these cases, it would have been better if the project had been done right in the first place or if it had not been started at all.

The "Not Invented Here" Syndrome

Ideas sometimes are not given a chance because of the "not invented here" syndrome. In this case, people from certain functional areas are resistant to ideas from other parts of the company. There are jealousies between the functional areas, and turf issues get in the way of progress. This problem is often a result of a phased approach to product development in which people don't hear about a project until it is handed off to them.

Using Multifunctional Teams for Every Project

It's possible to get carried away with the idea that multi-functional teams are good for product development, sometimes to the extent that the process is applied to *all* development projects, regardless of their size or complexity. In reality, there are some small and simple projects that will be inhibited by using a full multifunctional team approach. These projects are best done by just a few people who can run very fast and complete the project in a very short time. Be careful, though, because there are cases where what at first appeared to be a very small and simple project in reality became a complicated effort that should have been done by a full multifunctional team.

Overall Consideration

Because no company is perfect, there are bound to be barriers to new product development to some degree or another. Company management has to be vigilant in its search for barriers and take steps to eliminate them to the extent possible. Asking people at all levels within the company to identify the barriers as they perceive them is a healthy first step.

9 Uncovering Marketplace Needs

Company leaders fear that a lot of money will be spent on developing new products that don't sell once they are introduced into the marketplace. They fear that they may develop the wrong products or develop products with the wrong features. They worry that they may not know enough to pursue a good idea because they haven't identified a corresponding need in the marketplace.

These fears are more likely to come true if a company has poor awareness of the attributes and needs of its marketplace.

Understanding marketplace needs and developing products that satisfy those needs tilt the odds in favor of successful new product development.

THE ODDS OF SUCCESS

Even under the best of circumstances, not a whole lot of ideas for new products get anywhere within a company. Typically, with a phased approach to product development, out of 60 ideas starting into new product development, only 1 will become a commercial success in the marketplace.[1] With a multifunctional parallel approach, 1 out of 7 ideas typically makes it in the marketplace. Ideas fail as they go through the development cycle because they fail to pass various tests for soundness or because people lose interest.

There is nothing wrong with the fact that most ideas for new products fail early in the development cycle. In reality, only the very best ideas should make it to the marketplace. Otherwise, poor or marginal development projects would drain a company of its resources and prevent it from pursuing better opportunities. Poor projects need to be weeded out as early as possible.

HOW TO UNCOVER MARKETPLACE NEEDS

The fax machine was invented and developed in America, yet none of the fax machines now sold in the United States are American made. The U.S. companies that developed the fax machine convinced themselves that there was no market for the new product because they relied on faulty market research to measure potential consumer interest. They asked the wrong question.[2]

They went out and asked people if they would be interested in buying a device that would cost over \$1,500 and would send a letter at a cost of over \$1 per page, compared to the 25 cents per page that the post office was charging at that time. People answered with a resounding "No." Had they asked if people had a need for immediate delivery of letters, they would have gotten a different answer.

The Japanese, however, concentrated on understanding the *needs* of the marketplace. They went out and asked people if they had a need for the instant delivery of some of their letters. The answer was "Yes." Once they understood the need, the Japanese reasoned that people would buy a machine even if it cost \$1,500. They realized further that growth of courier services such as Federal Express had prepared the market for the fax machines.

Today, fax machines are everywhere: in offices, in homes, and even in cars. They have become a way of life. No doubt the need was there and the machine satisfied that need.

There is no single procedure that will provide all the information necessary to identify marketplace needs. Rather, it is a number of activities that, when examined collectively, begin to provide an understanding of the marketplace and its needs.

You need to learn as much as possible about the nature of your marketplace if you are going to develop credible new products. At very least, you need to know about

- Market trends
- Your customers' needs for new products or services
- Attitudes toward your products and your company
- Attributes of your customers
- Your customers' problems and concerns
- Information about your competition

Whatever methods are employed to study the marketplace, the information will be of far higher quality if R&D, engineering, manufacturing, and senior management people are active and willing participants in the process along with the sales and marketing people.

The following is a list of procedures that can help uncover important information about the marketplace.

FOCUS GROUP DISCUSSIONS

A focus group is a meeting of 8 to 12 target consumers who discuss a topic of particular and immediate interest to the company. It's a means of identifying the needs of that particular group. The discussion can focus on a current product, a concept, a prototype or model of a new product or a problem. Typically, it is a two-hour meeting that takes place at a facility where the proceedings can be observed behind a one-way mirror or can be videotaped for later viewing.

A focus group is a powerful means of uncovering consumer opinions. It often leads to ideas for new products. While focus groups usually are led by a trained facilitator, it is best if R&D, engineering, marketing, and manufacturing representatives listen in on the proceedings. When these people listen to the focus groups, they often come up with creative and innovative ideas for new products.

When Comet cleanser was introduced by Procter & Gamble, it contained an abrasive powder and it did not contain bleach. Later, a scientist was listening to a focus group that was discussing the use of the product. He heard one customer say that when she wanted to remove a particularly tough stain, she mixed a little bleach with the cleanser powder. This was the clue that the scientist needed, and he went on to make a version of Comet that contained bleach. Comet was able to take a dominant position in the marketplace because of information that was learned in a focus group.

Focus groups are not an end unto themselves. Rather, they are the first step in the search for marketplace needs. They do not yield quantifiable data because they are a small sample. However, they can provide insight into your customer's opinions, feelings, attitudes, and needs, especially those needs that are difficult to articulate clearly. Focus groups should always be followed up by quantitative research to answer other questions, such as market size, potential market share, competitive practices, and pricing.

Consider this word of caution about focus groups: if the product being discussed is totally new, it may be hard for respondents to render a valid opinion because they have nothing to relate it to. This is where the skills of a trained facilitator come into play and where it is particularly important that the material shown to the focus group attendees be developed very carefully. (See Chapter 7 for a discussion on a simplified approach to quality function deployment, a more effective way of conducting focus groups and identifying customer needs.)

TALKING TO THE CUSTOMERS

Nissan hires teams to go into U.S. homes with video cameras to talk to its customers. Interviewers ask the customers what they would like for new features for their cars. Nissan has gone so far as to hire anthropologists to find out what makes people buy cars. As a result of customer surveys in California, Nissan replaced pop-up headlights in its 300ZX with less obtrusive ones.

Mazda engineers study the relationship that exists between car design and human emotions. They monitor heart rate and breathing rates of drivers who describe their feelings as they drive along a test track.

After Honda listened to its customers, its design engineers redesigned its cars' door locks and turn signal indicators to give them a better feel.

Anybody can talk to the customers, not just the Japanese. Listening to the customers and making an active attempt to uncover their ideas, thoughts, and feelings is a powerful way of learning marketplace needs, no matter what business you are in. People are only too glad to have a chance to talk to you, provided you take the time to meet with them.

ANALYZING MARKETPLACE TRENDS

You need to develop an understanding of those changing environmental factors that are likely to influence your customers and your products. Changing life-styles, attitudes, population shifts, and social trends all influence the needs and wants of your customers.

For instance, a change in American life-style set the stage for the VCR that became so popular in this country. People began to lead far more active lives away from home, and many women began to work for the first time. This left people with less time at home to enjoy their favorite television programs. The VCR, with a timer that could be set to record programs while people were away from home, solved the problem.

Market trends are the least expensive aspect of the marketplace to study. Yet they have the greatest long-term impact on your current and future products. Most of the necessary information is readily available on electronic data bases and in magazines, reports, and other written materials. Key customers are often a source of information about market trends within their particular industries.

Companies that fail to spot a major marketplace trend can find themselves on very shaky ground. Toshiba missed the trend with its laptop computers when it failed to react in time to the marketplace need for notebook-size computers and computers with a faster chip. Toshiba let its technology get outdated, and while still a major contender in the laptop computer business, it lost market share unnecessarily.

THE KEY CUSTOMER

Key customers are particularly important to you if your products are in a rapidly changing field. Key customers are familiar with the conditions that exist in their marketplace. They have needs far sooner than anyone else, and they would benefit from new products that meet those needs. The task is to identify those needs and to develop new products that can satisfy those needs.[3]

Key customers can

- Identify important market trends
- Identify their needs for new products
- React to proposed solutions to their problems
- Test new products at the prototype stage
- Serve as members of a development team
- Identify other people you should talk to

The first step is to identify your key customers. They are not necessarily the company's largest customers. Cooperative suppliers, data bases, and information kept in your sales department are all sources of names of potential lead customers. Once you have the names, you can send them a questionnaire or use the telephone to determine which companies ought to be visited. A team consisting of people from R&D, Engineering, Marketing, Sales, and Manufacturing should then visit these customers.

When key customers are visited, they may not be very articulate when asked what their needs are. Further, they may be suspicious at first, until they realize that you can help them. You may have to sign a nondisclosure agreement before they are willing to discuss their needs.

IDENTIFYING PROBLEMS WITH CURRENT PRODUCTS

Too little effort is made to analyze problems that customers have with products. Yet this readily available information can be a powerful stimulus for innovative ideas for new products.

Keeping track of your customer's complaints and going out of your way to find out what is troubling them about your products will pay off. They'll be glad to talk to you and will often make suggestions for new products or for possible line extensions or modifications of your current product line.

After analyzing customer complaints, Procter & Gamble learned that consumers didn't like the cap on liquid detergent bottles because it became too messy after several uses. In response to this information, the company solved the problem by developing a new closure. It combined a measuring cup and draining device so that the cap could drain back into the container. This solution enabled Procter & Gamble to sell more Liquid Tide. The idea wouldn't have emerged if P&G hadn't made a point of paying attention to customer complaints.

LEARNING FROM SUPPLIERS

Suppliers are an excellent source of information about marketplace conditions. Since they are visiting you and your competition all the time, there is no reason why you can't learn from them. They can help identify market trends, provide information about the competition, identify potential customers, and suggest possible additions to your product lines. All you have to do is ask them their opinions, and they will oblige with plenty of useful information.

LEARNING FROM COMPETITORS

It appears as if we do our best to keep our heads in the sand when it comes to our competitors. Not only do we try to keep our secrets away from them, but we also exert very little effort to learn from them.

If you think about it, your competitors know as much about your marketplace as you do, or even more. This being the case, it makes sense to try to learn as much as you can from them. You can find out what they know about the marketplace by having your salespeople talk to their counterparts and by examining their products. Don't forget that the competition is probably watching you very closely and doing everything they can to learn what you know about the marketplace.

SYSTEMATICALLY COLLECTING DATA FROM CUSTOMER CONTACTS

Your customers contact you far more often than you think. You can learn a lot about the nature of the marketplace if you systematically keep track of every contact your company has with its customers. You can learn about marketplace trends and needs by analyzing customer questions, complaints, and concerns that came in on your 800 number; by examining returned warranty cards; and by keeping track of service calls and reorders.

IDENTIFYING GAPS IN THE MARKETPLACE

A marketplace gap analysis is a very useful way of identifying places in a marketplace niche where you don't now have a product and where you would benefit by having one. In a gap analysis you create a matrix, as follows:

- Across the top of a piece of paper, list all the market niches into which you could be selling your products. Assign a column for each niche.

- At the bottom of each column, list the total market potential of each niche, your prior year's sales into that niche and your percent market share.

- On the left side of the page, list all the possible products that can be sold into each of the niches.

- Inside the matrix, indicate all the products that are sold by you and your competition into each niche.

- Identify where there are gaps, that is, marketplace niches into which products are not being sold by you.

This exercise will help you identify possible products that you might want to develop or will promote ideas for new products that don't now exist at your company. It also will relate the potential new products to possible market share and will give you a far better idea of your competition's product lines.

DEVELOPING A MARKETING PLAN THAT IS UNDERSTOOD BY ALL

A workable and clearly understood marketing plan is an important aspect of the new product development process. It is a statement of how you plan to relate to your marketplace. It is unique to your company and, when completed, it is an action plan that will provide you with

- A mission statement
- Objectives and goals that can be measured
- General strategies for attaining each objective
- Specific tactics for each strategy

The marketing plan analyzes where you are now, where you will be in the future, and how your objectives, goals, strategies, and tactics will get you there.

Engineering, R&D, and manufacturing people should be allowed to help the marketing staff develop the marketing plan. Anything you can do to foster an understanding of the marketplace by the technical people will help assure that your new products actually relate to a real marketplace need.

MARKETPLACE PULL VERSUS TECHNOLOGY PUSH

Marketplace pull and technology push are terms that are used to describe whether a product was developed in response to a preconceived marketplace need or the result of a technical breakthrough in a laboratory.

- *Marketplace pull:* identifying a marketplace need and then developing a new product to meet that need.

- *Technology push:* identifying an interesting technology, making a product, and then searching for a marketplace.

Some companies are market driven while others are technology driven. Some claim that they are market driven, but they are actually sales or manufacturing driven; that is, they develop products that are based solely on customer requests or based on their manufacturing capabilities.

Market-driven companies are aware of their marketplace and try to develop products that meet the needs of that marketplace. They are concerned with growing their market share by concentrating on using the technologies they already have in-house or that are readily available from the outside.

Technology-driven companies look beyond the limitations imposed by their current technologies. They assume that the needs of tomorrow's customers will not be met with today's technologies. They try to develop new technologies without necessarily knowing what markets the products developed from these technologies will serve. They believe that, once the new technologies are developed, a search for market opportunities will yield commercially successful products.

Strictly market-driven companies have a risk of losing out when their market experiences a downturn because they will have no new technology available to enable them to move rapidly into other markets. They also have a greater risk that their competitors will pull ahead of them with a new product line that is driven by a new technology.

Strictly technology-driven companies have a greater risk that they will not find a market for their technologies and that they will have wasted all the time and money that went into the development of that technology. Such companies need to have big cash reserves, a lot of luck, and plenty of patience if they are to succeed by limiting themselves to this route.

No company needs to or should restrict itself to one approach or another. Market-driven companies can expand their horizons by moving into a broader technological base, and technology-driven companies can learn more about the marketplace and seek greater opportunities for their products. While most manufacturing companies need to concentrate on marketplace pull activities, they should not neglect to develop or acquire new technologies.

There are a number of cases where R&D developed products for which there was no known use in the marketplace at the time. Yet these products went on to become outstanding commercial successes. Some of these products are lasers, xerography, nylon, synthetic diamonds, germanium diodes, and fluorochemical polymers. It is worth examining several product developments that were driven by technology to see what lessons can be learned.

3M's Scotchgard

This is the case of a product that started out as a technology for which no market had yet been identified. In the 1950s, 3M had been committing major laboratory resources to conduct fluorochemical research.[4] While the firm had no particular application in mind, the researchers believed that this class of chemicals someday would have commercial value.

One of the earliest compounds made was a fluorochemical chrome complex, which the scientists quickly discovered would render a fabric sample repellent to water and oil. Unfortunately, this early version also turned every fabric with which it came in contact an odd shade of green. The scientists persisted, however. By then, they had begun to believe that there might be a use for a chemical compound that would render fabric impervious to dirt and grease, provided it didn't change the color of the fabric.

A number of other laboratory samples of fluorochemical compounds were made. One day, a technician spilled a dilute solution of a polymer on her sneakers. When she tried to rinse it off, she noticed that the color wasn't changed and that the water beaded up. She also noticed that over time the sneaker that had the polymer spilled on it remained clean while the other sneaker got dirty. This was hard evidence that 3M had the potential of making a commercially useful product from its fluorochemical research.

Continuing laboratory efforts refined the polymer into a stable emulsion. This material was introduced in 1958 as the first version of Scotchgard, a product that ultimately went on to major commercial success.

However, the new technology by itself wasn't enough to develop a market for the product. As is typically the case with a technology-driven new product, there was no understanding in the company or in the marketplace of its value. The product development team had to educate other people in the company, including the manufacturers and the sales force. The team also had to devise ways of educating the consumers on the value of waterproofing fabrics and making them repellent to grease and dirt. They had to create a market where none had existed before.

The scientists had to learn all about the manufacturing and usage of different kinds of fabrics. They visited fabric knitting mills, yarn producers, cutters, and others involved in the manufacturing of fabrics. They traveled to department stores, men's stores, women's dress shops, and others involved in the distribution chain. They also visited leading furniture, drapery, rainwear, and shoe manufacturers.

What started out as a monumental technology program ended up becoming an equally monumental marketing program. As usually happens with a product that started off being driven by technology, there had to be a conversion to marketplace pull for it to succeed.

It took 3M a huge amount of effort and plenty of money to learn about marketplace needs and to build consumer awareness about Scotchgard. All that work paid off. By 1987, it was estimated that Scotchgard had a 94% consumer awareness. By that time, the company had provided over 500 million tags that manufacturers attached to fabric and leather consumer goods.

Procter & Gamble's Crest Toothpaste

This product actually started out in 1934, when a traveling executive discovered alkyl sulfate in Germany and brought some back to the laboratory for the scientists to examine.[5] While it was known that alkyl sulfate had foaming qualities similar to soap, there was no known use in mind. It soon developed that alkyl sulfate was superior to soap in several ways: it could be used in hard water, it produced copious suds, and it was very soluble in water.

Three products were developed with alkyl sulfate, none of them a toothpaste. These were Dreft, a dry powder for washing dishes and clothes; Drene, a shampoo; and Teel, a liquid dentifrice.

In the early 1950s, the company decided that a toothpaste had to be part of its overall strategy to enter the personal products market. But, after the demise of Teel at about that time, it had no new products that would enable it to enter that market.

At about that time, P&G's scientists became aware of the possible use of fluoride as a decay preventive. It was based on an observation that tooth decay was minimal in a certain region of Texas where there was a high concentration of fluoride in the drinking water. This was further substantiated when it was found that dilute solutions of sodium fluoride would prevent tooth decay when applied topically to the teeth.

Soon thereafter, dentifrices containing alkyl sulfate were compounded with sodium fluoride, and when these were tested the initial results were encouraging. Later tests failed because the calcium compounds in the toothpaste reacted with the fluoride and rendered it inactive. Ultimately, a stable formulation was developed, and the toothpaste was found to prevent tooth decay.

It was clear to P&G that potential users of this product had no idea that it might be of value to them. They needed to be educated. It was believed that the best way to do that would be to get the approval of the Food and Drug Administration to conduct clinical trials and to get the endorsement of the American Dental Association once efficacy had been demonstrated.

P&G's scientists had to start by educating the FDA and then the ADA on the efficacy of their product. Trials began and the product was proven to be effective in preventing tooth decay. In 1959, the ADA gave Crest toothpaste its seal of approval. With that approval, Crest went on to capture significant market share.

KEY LESSONS FOR TECHNOLOGY-DRIVEN PRODUCT DEVELOPMENT

P&G's and 3M's experiences have taught many lessons on how to deal with products that are developed by the scientists for which there originally was little understanding of the needs of the marketplace. Some of these are

- Make sure top management is heavily involved in the project.

- Get the R&D professionals out into in the marketplace so they can learn firsthand about actual use conditions and possible alternative uses of their new product.

- Get the product out into test market as early as possible and get feedback from users. Developers often have to modify the technology extensively until there is a fit with the needs of the marketplace.

- Make sure R&D works hard to sell the idea for the new product to people within the company, especially those who are responsible for manufacturing and selling it. R&D personnel have to act as nonstop educators if the project is to succeed. Get other functional areas represented on the development teams as early as possible.

- With a technology-driven product, the end users usually will have no idea that the product will benefit them and they may not particularly care. They will need to be taught and the scientists should be involved in the process of educating them.

- Recognize that, after a while, a technology-driven product becomes pulled by the needs of the marketplace. Until this happens, the product is not likely to be a commercial success. The best situation is where technology push is converted to marketplace pull as quickly as possible.

Endnotes

[1] Booz, Allen & Hamilton, Inc. "New Product Development for the 1980's," 1982, in house report, New York.

[2] Peter Drucker, "Marketing 101 for a Fast-Changing Decade," *The Wall Street Journal,* November 20, 1990, p. A20.

[3] von Hippel, E. "New Product Ideas from 'Lead Users,'" *Research-Technology Management,* May/June 1989, pp. 82-96.

[4]LaZerte, D. J. "Market Pull/Technology Push," *Research-Technology Management,* March-April, 1989, pp. 25-29.
[5]Ibid.

10 Generating Ideas for New Products

New products are only as good as the idea upon which they are based: poor ideas will yield poor products, while products based on good ideas have a greater chance of performing well in the marketplace. It's important to examine the elements of idea generation. This chapter starts with definitions of the categories of new products, discusses the sources of ideas within companies and ways of improving the idea flow, and then offers criteria that can be used for the selection of projects.

CATEGORIES OF NEW PRODUCTS

According to a study by Booz, Allen & Hamilton,[1] there are six basic categories of new products, based on their newness to the company and their newness to the marketplace. These are

1. New-to-the-world products
2. New product lines
3. Additions to existing product lines
4. Improvements in or revisions to existing products
5. Repositionings
6. Cost reductions

New-to-the-World Products

These are products the company never made before and they create an entirely new category in the marketplace. It was estimated by Booz, Allen & Hamilton that this category represents 10% of all new product introductions. Examples of this category are the first Xerox copy machine, the first Polaroid camera, and the first facsimile machine.

New Product Lines

This category is made of new products that, while they are new to the company, are already being sold in the marketplace by other companies (20% of all new products). Examples include General Mills' and Kellogg's new cereals and Folger's new coffees.

Additions to Existing Product Lines

These are line extensions of products already made and distributed by the company (26% of all new products).

Improvements in or Revisions to Existing Products

These are replacements of existing products that offer improved performance or perceived greater value (26% of all new products).

Repositionings

This category is made of currently existing products that are targeted to new markets or new market niches (7% of all new products). Arm & Hammer's repositioning of its baking soda as a refrigerator deodorizer and later as a garbage grinder deodorant is an example of this category.

Cost Reductions

These are new products that deliver the same or better performance at a lower cost to the customer (11% of all new products).

A SIMPLIFIED VIEW

A much simpler way of categorizing new products is to divide them only into two categories, "new" and "market expansion" products.

New Product

By this definition, a "new" product is something that wasn't made yesterday and/or sold by the company, and it brings in new sales revenues.

Line extensions and product improvements become new products under the terms of this definition.

Market Expansion Product

Using this definition, if the product is exactly the same as one that is already being manufactured and sold by the company and if it satisfies the needs of a different marketplace niche or is a new application within the same niche, it is a "market expansion" product.

MAINTAINING A PORTFOLIO

Many companies never develop a product that is truly new, preferring instead to develop modifications and new applications of products that already exist. This may not be the safest approach in the long run because it rarely enables the company to take a commanding lead in the marketplace. Sooner or later, a competitor will be first in the market with a product that really does something new. When this happens, everyone else will be in a catch-up position for a long time to come.

It's important to minimize long-term risk. This can be done by maintaining a product portfolio that consists of a mix of different categories of products. A mixed portfolio consists of some products that are truly new to the company and the marketplace and others that are modifications and new applications of current products.

The ideal portfolio mix should be based on the average life cycles of the company's major product lines. For example, a company that has mostly products with long life cycles in its portfolio will need to have a lower percentage of new products than will a company whose products have relatively short life cycles.

THE IMPORTANCE OF KNOWING THE PERCENTAGE OF NEW PRODUCTS

Many leading manufacturing companies in the United States claim that 25 to 30 percent or more of current sales are from new products that were introduced in the prior five years.

Once a company knows what percentage of its current sales are from new products that were introduced in the prior five years and what its product portfolio mix is, it can compare itself to similar companies in its industry.

A discovery that its percentage of new product introductions is much lower than the industry average is a sign that the company is not spending enough time and money on new product development or that its new product development activities aren't effective. If it finds that this is the case, it can take steps to correct the situation.

GENERATING IDEAS FOR NEW PRODUCTS

An idea is a creative thought that leads to a proposal for a course of action. It is a delicate abstraction that is of value only when it is expressed. To survive, an idea needs to be exposed to the light of day in an environment that is healthy and supportive of its growth.

Any new product development project and its resulting product will be only as good as the original idea. At best, a mediocre idea will yield a mediocre product that will require extraordinary marketing and sales efforts if it is to generate any revenues.

A company that is lacking ideas for new products will find that its new product development program will never get off the ground. Because so many ideas fail to become commercially successful new products, there has to be plenty of ideas if the odds are going to be beaten.

Some companies seem to have more ideas than do others. If you look deeply enough, you will find that they have an environment that is particularly friendly to ideas for new products. Further, they are able to do something with the ideas once they have been expressed. They have a deliberate system in place for managing ideas, and they don't leave anything to chance.

The challenge of management, then, is to create an environment in which people are encouraged to submit their ideas, an environment in which ideas can grow into meaningful new products. There needs to be an active program for acquiring the ideas and for doing something with them once they enter the system.

MAKING IDEA MANAGEMENT SOMEONE'S RESPONSIBILITY

In most companies, idea handling is left entirely to chance. The company is lucky if a good idea somehow is submitted for consideration and even luckier if a good product is developed. Ideally, someone should be put in charge of the management of ideas. This person sets up a system for dealing with ideas and is responsible for

- Identifying the sources of ideas
- Stimulating ideas and seeking them out
- Notifying people that their ideas have been heard
- Cataloging ideas
- Getting ideas evaluated
- Reevaluating old ideas

This person can be the point source to whom everyone goes when he or she has a bright idea.

IDEAS FOR PRODUCTS VERSUS IDEAS FOR PROCESSES

Many of the ideas that come from Manufacturing, Engineering, R&D, and other technical sources will lead to projects that relate to process improvements. Because of their closer proximity to the marketplace, if Marketing, Sales, customers, suppliers, and distributors come up with ideas, the ideas will most likely lead to new products.

The easiest way to have technical people come up with more ideas for new products is to get them closer to the marketplace. To do this, they will need to visit customers, attend trade shows, observe customer focus groups, and spend more time with the salespeople and distributors.

WHERE DO IDEAS COME FROM?

Ideas for new products are not hard to find. The fact is that ideas are all around us all the time. It's just that we can't predict when they will come, where they will come from, or even whether we will recognize them when we see them.

Ideas come from

- Customers and prospects
- Sales representatives and distributors
- Technical staff
- Marketing staff
- Manufacturing staff
- Senior management and other staff
- Boards of directors and shareholders
- Suppliers
- Consultants and contract research companies
- Competitors
- Inventors
- Universities
- Technical and other publications
- Trade shows and conferences
- Guided brainstorming sessions

Most people have their brightest ideas away from the job environment. When asked, they will say that they do their best thinking while in the shower, while shaving, while in bed early in the morning or just before drifting off to sleep, in the car, and when out walking. Few people mention that they have great ideas while at work. They are too busy and they are not relaxed enough.

People will bring their bright ideas into the company when the work environment is healthy, high in energy, and safe and when they know that their ideas have a chance of getting somewhere.

A GOOD IDEA IS NO GUARANTEE OF SUCCESS

It's a mistake to think that a good idea for a new product is enough.

The idea must make business sense, and it must be developed into a product that meets marketplace needs, that can readily be manufactured, and that meets requirements for quality and profits. For a good idea to get anywhere, there must be a commitment to multifunctional parallel product development teams and an understanding that product features and design specifications must be frozen early.

"CHANCE FAVORS THE PREPARED MIND"

This quotation is attributed to Louis Pasteur, the famous French scientist. By this is meant that our minds have to be receptive to a stimulus before we can turn it into a bright idea. We also have to be willing to do something with the idea.

Alexander Fleming, a bacteriologist, noticed one day that green mold colonies seemed to inhibit the growth of nearby pathogenic bacterial colonies growing on the surface of a nutrient gel in a Petri dish. From this chance observation came his realization that the mold, later identified as a species of *Penicillium,* was giving off a chemical that killed bacteria or at least prevented their growth. The chemical later was called penicillin. This chance discovery, which happened to fall on a receptive mind, became the basis of the antibiotics industry.

Art Fry was in church one Sunday and he struggled to find a way to mark his place in a church hymnal. He was an employee of 3M, and he remembered that one of its scientists had developed an adhesive that had minimal sticking properties. One thought led to another and Fry later invented Post-it™ notepads, an extremely successful product line.

Edwin Land took his 3-year-old daughter for a walk. She asked him why she couldn't immediately see the pictures he had taken of her. He thought about her question and that line of thought led him to the concept of the instant camera and film.

IMPROVING THE FLOW OF IDEAS FROM CUSTOMERS

Customers can be a great source of ideas for new products. Many of them have a vested interest in the new product once it has been developed. In fact, for most companies, customers are usually the best source of ideas. Yet, many companies treat their customers in a very passive way. They depend on their sales force to pass along ideas when they hear of them, and they rarely seek out the ideas. There are ways of increasing the flow of ideas from customers.

Visit the Customers

The best people to visit the customers are those who are directly responsible for new product development; people from senior management, R&D, Engineering, Marketing, Sales, and Manufacturing. Visits can be set up in advance with key customers on their own turf. They can be given an opportunity to express their views of current products or products they would like to see developed.

Conduct Customer Focus Groups

Professionally facilitated customer focus groups can be an effective way of inviting customers to share their ideas for new products. To get the greatest yield from focus groups, they should be observed by the same people who have gone out to visit the customers, people from senior management, R&D, Engineering, Marketing, Sales, and Manufacturing. The focus groups can be observed behind one way mirrors or, at very least, audio- or videotapes of the sessions can be made and listened to later.

Focus groups often concentrate on currently available products. These discussions can lead to suggestions for improvements and to ideas for new products. (See Chapter 7 for a description of a simplified approach to quality function deployment, a process that uses focus groups.)

Listen to Customer's Suggestions on Solving Problems

Customers who have problems with your products often are very good at suggesting ways of solving the problems. It's important to tap into this reservoir of ideas. Some companies go so far as to install a telephone 800 hot line that is dedicated to listening to customer's suggestions for the solutions to product problems.

Ask the Customers for Advice

When Boeing wanted help in figuring out how to design its new 777 wide-bodied two-engine passenger jet, it turned to eight of its potential customers for help.[2] Boeing invited ideas from American, United, British Airways, Delta, Japan Airlines, Qantas, All Nippon, and Cathay Pacific.

The plane's design plans, when finalized, will include the features the customers wanted. It will have seating for 360 people, two fuel-efficient and quiet engines, folding wingtips to reduce the 196-foot wingspan to 156 feet, and instrumentation that makes it possible to use two pilots instead of three. The airplane will also have flexible design, so that its galleys, lavatories, and seats can be moved about on tracks, enabling the airline to change the plane's configuration easily.

Asking your customers for advice is a good way of making sure that your products meet their needs. It greatly improves the odds that your new product will capture market share once it is developed and released.

IDEAS FROM THE COMPETITION

The competition is a source of ideas for new products that often is overlooked. Knowledge of the competition's products often stimulates ideas that lead to the development of products that have superior features and that meet a definite marketplace need.

It's not difficult to tap into this source of information from the competition. What is needed is an awareness of who the competitors are and the nature of their product lines. Many companies get ideas for new products by studying samples of a competitor's product.

IDEAS FROM TRADE SHOWS AND PROFESSIONAL MEETINGS

Trade shows and professional meetings are far more than marketing opportunities or social events. They are places for people to learn and to share thoughts. They enable people to make new connections in their minds and to come up with ideas they never would have thought of otherwise.

There are plenty of trade shows, and the first step is to identify those that are relevant. At least one key person should be sent to each of these shows.

Attendees should receive training on what to look for, which exhibits should not be missed, and how to keep records on what they have seen and heard. They should know that, while the trade show is an opportunity to socialize and have fun, it is a good time to learn and to think of ideas for new products. To do this, they will have to visit all the booths, talk to a lot of people, listen to presentations, and study the competition.

Trade shows are often good places to learn of customer response to newly released products.

People who attend trade shows should be required to make a presentation on what they have learned and to talk about their ideas for possible new products soon after they return to the company. This offers those who had to stay home exposure to new information, and it gives them a chance to come up with their own ideas for new products.

Attendance at trade shows is hard work, but it pays off with many ideas for credible new products.

IDEAS FROM SUPPLIERS

Suppliers, especially large ones, are good sources of ideas for new products. Because their salespeople travel widely among their territories, they have an excellent idea of marketplace trends and competitor plans. They have a vested interest in selling their products to you and are often willing to share the results of their own R&D and Engineering work facilities. Key suppliers can often help in the development of a new product by suggesting which of their products or services ought to be used, provided they are brought into a product development project early enough.

Marketing and technical people should visit key suppliers regularly to learn about new materials and products and to talk about ideas for new products.

IMPROVING THE FLOW OF IDEAS FROM WITHIN THE COMPANY

Potentially, every employee within a company is an excellent source of ideas for new products. Yet people are often overlooked. Senior managers often think that their employees have no creative ideas or that the ideas are unrelated to the needs of the business. If there is an element of truth to some of these negative assumptions, it is because management has not taken positive steps to provide an environment that is conducive to idea generation or to tell its people what the company is trying to achieve.

Management can take definite steps to improve the quality and quantity of ideas for new products. Some of these steps are

- Make sure everyone in the company knows the company's mission, objectives, and goals so that they will know what kinds of ideas to submit.

- Let people know that their ideas are wanted and make sure that people who submit ideas receive timely recognition. Make an effort to identify all possible sources of ideas.

- Appoint a person to be in charge of the management of ideas.

- Make sure that technical people are exposed to the customers and have them observe focus groups where customers talk about their needs.

- Set up a small multifunctional team to evaluate ideas.

- Encourage attendance at trade shows and professional meetings.

- Reward the person who had the good idea that benefited the company.

- Use guided brainstorming techniques to generate many ideas for new products in a short time.

- Reexamine shelved ideas at regular intervals to find those whose time has come.

- Establish a companywide idea pool that people can tap into for ideas for new products.

GUIDED BRAINSTORMING

Guided brainstorming is a technique that is used to generate a large number of ideas in a very short period of time. At a guided brainstorming session, it's not unusual for hundreds of ideas to be generated by a small group of people in several hours or less. A guided brainstorming session uses the services of a trained facilitator to run the sessions and to manage the follow-up activities.

Guided brainstorming sessions are designed to promote divergent as opposed to convergent thinking. Divergent thinking is highly creative, is imaginative, and produces many ideas. Convergent thinking is more focused and analytical, is logical, and produces a few specific solutions to specific problems.

When conducting a brainstorming session, there are some basic rules that should be followed and the people who participate must be thoroughly aware of the rules. The rules for a brainstorming session are

- Any idea is appropriate.
- The more ideas, the better.
- Judgment is not allowed.

A brainstorming session, if successfully run, is a very high energy and freewheeling experience for the participants, a time for them to be very creative and to have fun.

Brainstorming sessions work best with fewer than 20 people. They should take place in a comfortable setting where there are no telephone interruptions. It's best if they take place in the morning while people are wide awake. The basic steps to a brainstorming session are

1. Explain the rules and stress the need to be nonjudgmental.
2. Conduct a warm-up exercise, for example, "How many uses can we think of for this object (e.g., a paper clip) within five minutes?"
3. State the problem, for example, "How many ideas for a new product that will help meet our customer's needs can we think of?"
4. Record the ideas on a flipchart and post the sheets of paper on the wall.
5. Don't run a brainstorming session too long. Two hours seems to be the time it takes to reach intellectual and creative exhaustion.

Follow-up to the brainstorming session is an important step. There are several approaches to this:

1. A small team reviews the list of ideas and narrows them down to 40 or 50 candidates. These ideas are then sent to all the participants in the brainstorming session. People are then given five business days to rank order the ideas and to return their lists to the team. The returns are analyzed, and the top four or five ideas are identified. The participants are then notified of the results. The small team selects the idea they wish to pursue, and the work begins.

2. Alternatively, each person attending the brainstorming session is given five colored stickers. After all the ideas have been generated, people are asked to walk around the room and place their stickers alongside each of their five favorite ideas. It then becomes a fairly simple matter to look for the clusters of stickers. The members of the small team referred to earlier still have to select the idea they like best.

Either approach works, although there is a greater opportunity for people to submit additional ideas if the first approach is followed.

A brainstorming session should never be done if there is no intention of doing something with the best idea. If people have participated in a brainstorming session and have gone out of their way to evaluate the ideas, they will be thoroughly disheartened if nothing comes of their work. They will feel cheated and will be less likely to participate enthusiastically in later sessions.

SETTING UP A COMPANYWIDE IDEA BANK

Setting up a computerized data base of ideas can be a helpful way of increasing the chances that a good idea will not be lost. With an idea bank, all ideas for new products and those ideas that were shelved are logged into a computer data base, and they are cross indexed by a number of attributes: their market niche, the technology required, type of product, the name of the person who had the idea, and the date the idea was logged in.

Whenever anyone is looking for an idea that may meet certain characteristics, it becomes a simple matter to check in with the idea bank to see if there is an idea that might fit the current need. If there is, a quick telephone call to the originator of the idea can yield a lot of information in a short time, and it may even identify a potential member of the new product development team.

EXAMINING SHELVED IDEAS

Most companies have a number of ideas that were considered at one time and, for any of a number of reasons, were found to be unacceptable. These shelved ideas, if retained and reexamined periodically, can be a potential source of ideas for successful new products. An idea that was no good in yesterday's environment might be appropriate today because of changes in the marketplace, the appearance of a new customer need, the availability of resources, or recent advances in technology.

ESTABLISHING CRITERIA FOR THE SELECTION OF PROJECTS

Why Criteria Are Needed

New product development is a gamble, even under the best of circumstances. At one time it was appropriate to decide whether to go forward with a development project by "gut feel." Now, however, the marketplace and competitive situation have gotten so complicated and the cost of development projects has gotten so expensive that a more sophisticated means of evaluating and selecting projects is necessary.

You can improve the odds of success by selecting better projects and by weeding out, as early as possible, those ideas that make little sense to pursue. Listing criteria for the evaluation and selection of development projects is a way of improving the odds. Seeing how well a project meets preestablished criteria is an important way of determining whether a project is worth starting or continuing.

Criteria are qualitative and quantitative lists of attributes that address marketing, financial, technological, manufacturing, and competitive advantage issues. Well-thought-out criteria

- Provide guidelines that can be used to determine whether a project should be started

- Provide guidelines that can be applied at critical project milestones to determine whether a project should be continued
- Let people know how their ideas will be evaluated and help steer the types of ideas so that they are more likely to meet the needs of the company

Who Prepares the Criteria

Criteria are best prepared by a team consisting of management representatives from senior management, Marketing, Sales, R&D, Engineering, Manufacturing, and Finance. These people are in the best position to understand the needs of the company and they are the most likely to evaluate ideas for potential projects.

Criteria should be updated annually to reflect changing market conditions and company circumstances. The criteria should be circulated to everyone in the company who has anything to do with new product development.

Criteria as Guidelines

Criteria are meant to be guidelines. They are not rigid rules that are never meant to be broken. The danger in getting too serious about the application of criteria is that it is possible to miss out on good ideas that meet most but not all of the criteria.

Elements of the Criteria

New product criteria address a number of important issues:

- Fit within the company's business and culture
- Compatibility with the company's core technologies
- Compatibility with the company's marketplace niche
- Ability to satisfy a specific customer need
- Possibility of achieving major market share
- Potential sales and profits
- Net present value return
- Time for payback of development costs

- Cost of major tooling and machinery
- Internal rate of return on the investment
- Susceptibility to competitive attack
- Fit within the capabilities of existing and contemplated staff
- Growth potential of the product line
- Possibility of follow-on products
- Likelihood of being first in the marketplace with the new product
- Possibility of catching the competition by surprise
- Location of the market (local, national, or international)
- Existence of a channel to the marketplace
- Potential downside risks of proceeding
- Potential risks of not proceeding
- Possible synergistic effect with current product lines
- Existence of identified lead customers
- Development cost and time
- Existence of a product champion
- Patentability and trade secrecy
- Likelihood that the new product will provide distinct competitive advantages to the company
- Availability of technology
- Resources required
- Ability to leverage available technology
- Urgency and criticality
- Uniqueness
- Technical merit
- Speed of entry into the marketplace
- Possibility of creating or dominating a niche market

Obviously, not all these criteria are important for every company. Some are more important than others. It is up to each company to decide which of these must be met by a proposed project before it is allowed to go forward. The company should divide its list of criteria into subcategories: those that are absolutely essential for all of its projects and those that are less important.

Sometimes, the criteria take the form of a checklist that is used when evaluating potential projects. Figure 10.1 is an example of such a checklist

Figure 10.1
Potential New Product Checklist

Marketing/Sales	Yes	No	Maybe
Is there a marketplace need for this product?			
Does the customer need already exist?			
Will the consumers pay to satisfy this need?			
Can we be first in the marketplace with this product?			
Are there barriers to entry that can be erected?			
Does it fit our current markets?			
Does it fit into our channels of distribution?			
Can it be sold effectively with our existing sales force?			
Does it fit our marketing strategy?			
Can we be a low-cost producer of this product and/or a differentiated supplier?			

Design/Development/Manufacturing			
Does it fit with our core technologies?			
Is it technically innovative?			
Is it readily manufacturable?			
Can we manufacture it with our current facilities?			

	Yes	No	Maybe
Do we have the resources to do this project?	___	___	___
Are we better off acquiring the product?	___	___	___
Can we develop a high-quality product quickly and still meet marketplace needs in time?	___	___	___
Can there be follow-on products?	___	___	___

Financial

	Yes	No	Maybe
Is the magnitude of this opportunity sufficient?	___	___	___
Does it meet our minimum quantity requirements?	___	___	___
Are the market projections reasonable?	___	___	___
Are the development costs reasonable?	___	___	___
Can the initial investment be minimized?	___	___	___
Will it require a minimal capital investment?	___	___	___
Will it meet return-on-investment targets?	___	___	___

Other

	Yes	No	Maybe
Does it fit our corporate objectives?	___	___	___
Does it fit or enhance the company's image?	___	___	___
Are there insignificant regulatory or compliance problems?	___	___	___
Are there major risks if we do not proceed with this project?	___	___	___
Are there few major risks if we do proceed with this project?	___	___	___
Is there a potential proprietary position?	___	___	___
Is there a product champion?	___	___	___

Competitive Advantages

A new product should confer a number of competitive advantages upon the company, for example, it

- Can be developed and deployed into the marketplace very rapidly
- Fits within a current distribution network
- Can dominate a marketplace niche
- Can be sold with a healthy gross margin
- Offers distinct advantages over existing products
- Provides significant barriers to entry for potential competitors
- Enhances the prestige of the company
- Provides an opportunity for spin-off products
- Can attract the interest and enthusiasm of a key customer
- Adds significantly to other product lines through synergistic effects
- Has patentability or trade secrecy

If a potential new product cannot meet at least two thirds of the listed competitive advantages, it might not be worth doing the development project.

RULES OF THUMB FOR MINIMIZING RISK

Maintaining a project portfolio that consists of a mix of different types and sizes of projects will minimize risk and will improve the chances that more new and successful products will make it to the marketplace.

Selecting projects that meet the criteria established for the company and that confer distinct competitive advantages will help reduce risk. A project that is based on meeting well-defined customer needs is more likely to succeed, particularly if it is developed by a multifunctional team with an experienced leader.

Generally, there is less risk in introducing new products into current markets than there is in introducing products into markets that are new to the company. There also is less risk when the new product offers higher value to the customers than any other product already in the marketplace.

Endnotes

[1]Booz, Allen & Hamilton, "New Product Management for the 1980's," 1982, in house report, New York.

[2]"New Boeing Airliner Shaped by the Airlines," *The New York Times*, 12/19/90, p. C1.

11 Team Management and Team Leadership

THE NEED FOR TEAMS

Major new product development projects have become much too complex to be completed successfully by any one individual or by a single functional department. It's been realized by successful companies that it takes good teamwork to develop good products. Multifunctional teams pool the collective skills, knowledge, experience, and training of all participants and make fast new product development possible.

Good teamwork requires an enthusiastic and deep commitment from senior management and from the functional department heads. They must truly be believers in the team concept. Teams will work well only if they have the right players and only if they are managed effectively by qualified leaders.

Ideally, a team works together to develop its objectives (based on management's definition of the project mission) and it has a vision of what needs to be accomplished. Its members believe the project can be done, they have a clear understanding of their goals, they know how to attain them, and they understand how teams work.

TEAM MEMBERSHIP

At a minimum, new product development teams should have people from Marketing, Sales, R&D, Design, Engineering, and Manufacturing. A well-rounded team should also have people from Finance, Quality Assurance, Purchasing, and anyone else who can make a significant contribution to the program. Key suppliers and, sometimes, key customers should also be represented on the teams. The team members should all start with the project at the same time at the beginning of the project. Ideally, company management selects the first few members of a new product development team from a group of volunteers. The rest of the team members are then chosen by the team itself and the team then chooses its own leader.

GUIDELINES FOR SUCCESSFUL TEAM MANAGEMENT

Having a Vision of the Project

Successful team management starts with clearly defined project objectives, that is, what the project hopes to accomplish, what milestones it will attain, and when it will meet them. It requires a clear understanding of who will be responsible for each of the individual tasks that are necessary to complete the project. Without a clear vision of the project, it will be difficult for the team to know when the project is completed.

Specific project objectives and milestones should not be imposed on the team by management. Teams should negotiate project objectives and milestones with management at the beginning of the project. Priorities should be reasonable, and project objectives should be revised only in response to changing company priorities.

Team members are more likely to feel ownership, pride, and a sense of urgency when they have helped to shape the project. Team members have a lot to do, and they need to know where the project is headed. They are responsible for many things, some of which are

- Identifying project milestones
- Ensuring timely completion of assigned tasks
- Identifying problems and concerns

- Seeking input from outside experts
- Communicating team activities with other employees and with each other
- Sharing their knowledge and expertise
- Participating in meetings and discussions
- Participating in presentations to management

Team Empowerment

Along with its responsibilities, a team should be given full authority to accomplish its goals. Senior management should be part of the goal setting at the early stage of the project. Once this has happened, the team should then be allowed to proceed from one milestone to another without being bothered and, other than keeping them informed, should only have to go to senior management for major capital approval. The team leader should be held accountable for reaching the milestones, and there should be reviews with senior management at significant intervals.

New product development is speeded up by adequately empowered teams because they have to spend less time seeking approval for their actions. Empowerment means that teams are given the right to make whatever decisions are necessary to complete the job, within preagreed spending and other guidelines. Such decisions may even include the right to select team members and to eject individuals who are not doing their fair share.

Team Size

An overly large team is hard to manage. It results in projects that take too long or that may not be completed. Little ever gets accomplished and team members are frustrated. Ideally, the teams should be small: 6 to 12 key players is best since it gets harder to communicate as the team gets larger.

A relatively small team is easier to manage. There is less conflict, there can be a clear definition of each member's role, and every member can be held accountable for the timely completion of tasks.

Keep in mind, though, that while the core team may consist of

6 to 12 key people, the actual team probably is much larger. Each core team member supervises the work of a number of other people, each of whom then becomes a member of the team. These support people are often forgotten when the project is successful.

Team Support

Moral support from upper management is not enough. To function well, teams need to be given the proper tools, equipment, and resources. They should have access to computer-aided design (CAD) equipment, materials, tools, 3-D modeling, workspace, personal computers, and any other resources that will make their work easier.

Access to Information

Communication is very important. If new product development teams are to succeed, they must have direct access to information and resources from all parts of the company and from outside the company as well. They cannot be isolated or left out of the communications loop.

Critical Path Project Management

Teams should be provided with critical path charting software that will enable them to

- List the tasks that need to be accomplished
- Develop a project schedule
- Understand project milestones
- Estimate resources required
- Know when the project is in trouble

The use of critical path project management will make it possible for the team, and senior management as well, to know where the project is at all times and to understand the effect of changes in the schedule on the overall project. (See Chapter 6 for more information on critical path project management.)

Co-location of Team Members

A team will function best if its members are not separated from each other by great distances. Ideally, to facilitate communication, team members should be in the same location. When there is too much distance between people, they spend too much time traveling back and forth and too little time working together. The best situation is one in which team members are concentrated in one area of one building with close proximity to the model shop and the manufacturing plant.

Team Unity

A team needs to work well together and to have team spirit. Team members need to know how their individual work can contribute to the team's success, each other's success, and the company's success. They need to give up the idea that they must compete against each other, and they need to work together for a common goal.

Good team spirit is more likely to develop in a company whose management is enthusiastically supportive of its teams and whose culture supports the concept of fast product development. There are times in any project when the going gets tough, and these are the moments when plenty of team spirit is needed to keep the project on track.

Simple things help develop team spirit. Team logos on coffee mugs, sweatshirts, and hats, team outings, and other events all help develop a sense of unity for the team and develop ownership and pride in the team. Teams that have found a way to play together build cohesiveness, have more energy and can vent their feelings.

Team unity is enhanced when a team that has agreed on its objectives and milestones has participated in setting them. The objectives and milestones should be written down and distributed to all the members of the team. When the group takes time to celebrate the completion of each major milestone, team spirit is developed further, and there is greater team enthusiasm.

A project ought to have a name that helps promote team spirit, and it is best if the team chooses the name. At Ingersoll-Rand, the development project for a new air grinder was called "Operation Lightning." This was a multifunctional team effort that developed a completely new tool in just one year, a remarkable effort considering the complexity of the project.

Good teams will develop their own rituals and protocols, such as celebrating birthdays and holidays, going out for a pizza or a few beers on certain occasions, greeting new members, or having a party for departing members. A team will develop a backlog of shared experiences and will have a history that helps create bonding among its members.

Ordinarily, high spirit will develop by itself in a well-run team that is meeting its objectives and is doing something important for the company. Little needs to be done to help the process along under those circumstances. In the long run, nothing helps develop team spirit more than success.

PART-TIME TEAM MEMBERSHIP

It's unusual for team members to be dedicated to only one project. In most companies, team members have other assignments as well. Sometimes, they are members of several development teams at the same time. If team members have been assigned unrealistic work loads, the teams will suffer and development projects won't be completed on time.

It isn't absolutely necessary for team members to have only one assignment. In fact, an argument can be made that multiple assignments are helpful in the long run, provided the work load doesn't become excessive. When, as often happens, the person encounters a problem for which a solution can't be found immediately, being able to go off and do something else for a while can be helpful. Often, the solution comes to the person while doing something totally unrelated.

GROUND RULES FOR TEAM OPERATION

Teams should be allowed to manage themselves, and, as early as possible in the process, the team should devote time to establishing a code of behavior for its members. Such ground rules help to prevent future problems because all team members know what is expected of them.

A team's ground rules might comprise the following:

- Attend all meetings or send a qualified alternate.
- Be on time for meetings.
- Initiate discussions.
- Respect the views of others.
- Come prepared to meetings.
- Seek information and opinion.
- Don't be critical or sarcastic.
- Complete assignments on time. Suggest ways of solving a problem or reaching a goal.
- Don't change the subject.
- Compromise and be willing to resolve differences.
- Accept and support the results of team decisions.
- Participate fully and enthusiastically.
- Pay attention at meetings.
- Seek consensus.
- Have a regular meeting time and place.
- Have team leader set the meeting's agenda.
- Circulate the agenda prior to the meeting.
- Keep meetings short and tightly focused.
- Keep minutes of all meetings.
- Define responsibilities.
- Keep cool and don't lose your temper.
- No smoking at meetings.
- Be open to suggestions.
- Respect the need for confidentiality.
- Everyone is equal during team meetings.
- Don't interrupt when someone is talking.
- Be fair.
- Be cooperative.

Generally, teams function best when everyone's talents are used, when everyone understands what is expected of them, and when they know who is responsible for the completion of each task.

THE TEAM LEADER

The choice of the team leader is very important, often making the difference between success and failure of a project.

The team leader has a lot to do. The leader must motivate, manage, and teach the members of a team. The leader should be someone with a strong personality, yet not be a dictatorial manager. The leader must be able to build trust among the team members and, at the same time, be trusted by senior management.

Ideally, the team leader seeks to bring out the best performance of the people within the team. The team leader acts as a general contractor.

The team leader has to understand that management by consensus is the best way to assure completion of the development project.

The best team leaders have

- A clear vision of the product
- Political savvy
- Dedication
- Good people management skills
- Plenty of energy
- Good understanding of the marketplace need
- General knowledge of the technologies involved
- Credibility with the team membership
- Good writing skills
- Oral presentation skills
- Good understanding of cash flow management
- An ability to roll with the punches

Ideally, the leader is someone who is selected by the team itself. When the team leader is appointed by management, it is less likely that the leader will be readily accepted by the team members.

To succeed, the team leader has to have a clear mandate from senior management and has to have support at all stages of the project.

Incidentally, nowhere is it written that the team leader has to be from the Engineering, Marketing, or any other functional area within the company. It actually matters very little where the leader comes from, provided the person has the right skills and has been selected by the team.

REWARDING TEAMS

Team rewards are an important way of building team unity and spirit, helping team members develop an emotional stake in the outcome of the product. Teams that are rewarded at the completion of key project milestones will continue to be highly motivated to succeed.

It is better to reward the whole team for exemplary performance than it is to reward individuals. Singling out and rewarding the star performers creates jealousies and friction within the team, and this gets in the way of progress.

There are many ways of rewarding a team. Generally, recognition is the best team reward, even better than money, provided people are adequately paid in the first place. Possible rewards for team recognition might include

- Broad coverage within the company publications
- Plaques of commendation
- Letters from senior management
- Visits to trade shows and professional meetings
- Paid vacations

A good way to identify rewards that will appeal to the team is to let the team decide for itself what it would like for rewards. It's good also for a team when it is surprised with a considerate reward from senior management.

When considering rewards for a team, it pays to include the spouses and other family members in the reward. Keep in mind that while the development project is moving along in high gear, these people are at home and are being denied the company and attention of the team members.

TEAM TRAINING

No amount of training will produce long-term beneficial effects if the teams have not been given clear operating guidelines and support from senior management. Usually, harmonious and effective team operation is the result of such support, not the result of exercises in team management or participation.

That being said, however, there still is room for team training. Such training should not be viewed as a quick fix but, rather, as one aspect of the support provided by management.

Team training can be helpful to the team effort, particularly with regard to teaching problem-solving methods, idea generation, group process, and communication. The team leader can draw upon internal and external resources to provide training programs that build on the current skills of the team members.

POTENTIAL PROBLEMS WITH TEAM MANAGEMENT

A team does not always work well. There will be trouble if it experiences frequent changes in direction, if it has rancorous discussions about task assignments, if its members feel that the project is more than they can handle, if they believe that the project is unimportant, and if they worry about lack of progress. Teams can feel helpless and not know where to turn for help.

Some of the other problems experienced by troubled teams include

- Bogging down with details
- Hidden agendas
- Poor leadership
- One person dominating meetings
- Lack of trust
- Unclear objectives and goals
- Poor planning
- Negative attitudes
- Team members having too many other responsibilities
- No clear definition of roles

- Failure to discuss
- Lack of support by higher authority
- Incomplete team
- Overrepresentation in any one area
- Team members not completing their tasks
- Unrealistic time schedules
- Inadequate resources
- Poor communication and documentation
- Personality conflicts
- Lack of consensus
- Failure to freeze the product features or design specifications
- Unresolved interfunctional conflicts
- Lack of direction by the leader
- Team size too large or too small
- Team members located too far apart

DISSOLVING THE TEAMS

It's a mistake to dissolve a development team too soon. Teams should not be dissolved until some time after the new product is being manufactured. There are bound to be problems, and the original development team is best equipped to handle them quickly and effectively.

As a rule of thumb, it would be appropriate to dissolve the development team after initial production problems have decreased to a level that is easily managed by production personnel.

WRAPPING IT UP

Teams seem to function best when the following conditions are met:

- They are supported by senior management.
- They have a clear vision of where they are going.
- They share in the objective and milestone setting and they use critical path project management.

- There is clear and open communication between the team members and management.
- They have all the right players from the different functions, all starting with the project from the start.
- They are adequately rewarded.
- The team's code of behavior is established by the team and it is clearly understood.
- There is equitable and balanced distribution of the work.
- Functional managers no longer see team operation as an encroachment on their turf.
- Team members are located near each other.
- The team is empowered.
- The team is not too large or too small.
- There is a healthy team spirit.
- The team leader is highly qualified.
- There is a product champion at a high enough level within the company.
- They are working in an environment where it is safe to make mistakes and have failures.
- The team is not dissolved too soon after the project is completed.
- The team realizes that the competition is outside the company and team members are all pulling together to achieve a common goal.

FORGING THE LINK BETWEEN TECHNICAL AND MARKETING PEOPLE

The Need to Forge the Link

Many technological developments never become new products because the technical people have no way of communicating their discoveries to the marketing and sales people or of finding out whether there is an actual marketplace need. Similarly, marketing people often have great ideas for new products and have no way of communicating their ideas to engineering, R&D, and manufacturing people. It's as if they are all speaking different languages.

Many great ideas never get off the ground because of lack of communication, a problem often based on misconceptions and mistrust between two opposing camps within the same company, technical people, and marketing people. Products that are developed by technical people without good marketing input don't have a high probability of success.

Fast parallel new product development will succeed only to the extent that technical and marketing people are capable of working well together in an atmosphere of harmony, trust, and respect.

Misconceptions About Each Other

Technical and marketing people have some astonishing misconceptions about each other. These are deep seated impressions that can be dislodged only with great difficulty.

Marketing people often think that technical people

- Have no sense of time
- Don't care about costs
- Have no idea of the real world
- Hide in the laboratory
- Can't communicate clearly
- Should be kept away from the customers
- Are very conservative
- Have a very narrow view of the world
- Always underestimate costs
- Have no sense of humor
- Are off in another world
- Are passive
- Don't understand customers
- Can't stick to schedules
- Are interested only in technology
- Are slow
- Never finish developing a product

Because of such misconceptions, technical people are often intentionally kept away from the customers. This keeps them further isolated and out of touch with the real world. As a result, their ideas for new products are even less likely to match real needs of the marketplace.

Technical people often think that marketing people

- Want everything now
- Are aggressive and too demanding
- Are unrealistic
- Can't make up their minds
- Change the design specifications frequently
- Are too impatient
- Are more interested in playing golf
- Are always in a hurry
- Don't trust technical people
- Set unrealistic goals for profit margins
- Cannot possibly understand technology
- Are not interested in the scientists' or engineers' problems
- Want to ship products before they are ready

As a result of such misconceptions, marketing people are often intentionally kept in the dark about developing technologies that might yield exciting new products. They are less likely to be able to respond to the needs of a changing marketplace because they have no idea of what might be possible. Further, they are likely to be blind-sided by a competitor who may be more capable of converting new technologies into saleable products.

The Kernel of Truth

There usually is a kernel of truth to the misconceptions. There really are differences between technical and marketing people. After all, it was more than just chance that led them to choose their professions in the first place. Personality traits had a lot more to do with their career path than anything else. In reality, technical people do tend to be less concerned with deadlines and more conservative, while marketing people do tend to be more flamboyant and less conservative.

Because they have distinctly different personalities, these people tend to react differently to the same stimuli. They don't understand each other, and they are driven by different motivations. They are inclined not to trust each other, and each tends to live in a world of isolation.

If these misconceptions are added to the normal barriers that are present in most companies, it's a wonder that any new product development occurs at all or that there is ever any meaningful dialogue between marketing and technical people.

The Need for Harmony

Obviously, no amount of harmony will help if a company doesn't have good ideas for new products, or it doesn't have a program for fast parallel product development, or it doesn't have adequate manufacturing capabilities. Conversely, even with good ideas for new products, multifunctional teams in place, and outstanding manufacturing capabilities, a lack of harmony between technical and marketing people will make it virtually impossible to conduct effective product development.

Even after new products have been developed, internal fighting makes it less likely that technical people will hear of opportunities for additional follow-on products or that they will share their bright ideas with the marketing people.

Any energy that goes into internal squabbling diminishes a company's chances of developing new products that do well in the marketplace.

Communication Means Talking

Memos erect barriers to communication. In fact, most memos are defensive documents designed to protect the writer in the event of a future conflict. Most memos are hard to read, say very little, and fail to accomplish anything of value.

If people want to relate well, they need to *talk* to each other, as often and as much as possible. A memo or an electronic message can never be a substitute for a meaningful conversation because it imposes a paper or computer screen barrier that is difficult to overcome.

Face-to-face conversations make it possible for each participant to detect and react to body language, facial expressions, tone of voice, and other clues, all of which communicate information about the other person. Subtle word meanings and expressions of interest or lack of interest are less likely to be missed.

Team training in group interaction and communication at the beginning of a new project is helpful. If done with sensitivity, such group training enables people to talk to each other and to begin to understand where each is coming from.

Shared Experiences as the Bridge

When marketing and technical people are isolated from each other, they are more likely to experience mutual distrust and disrespect.

They will begin to talk to each other when they understand each other's needs, motivations, and interests. A good way to achieve this is for the team to have shared experiences. If technical people are encouraged to go into the marketplace and if marketing people visit the laboratories and the manufacturing floor, they will begin to have shared experiences.

Transferring people from one department to another for short periods of time is another way of learning about each other. The old adage that you don't know very much about another person's problems until you have walked in his (or her) shoes still holds.

The Japanese Approach

In Japanese companies, technical people interact with marketing people to a far greater degree than is the case at American companies. At Hitachi, the technical staff meets at regularly scheduled monthly intervals with the marketing people to discuss progress and to learn what marketing considers the most promising new areas for further development.

There also is a greater degree of camaraderie between Japanese technical and marketing people than is the case in the United States. In Japan, these relationships go well beyond the normal interactions that occur during the working day. Japanese technical and marketing people develop a personal relationship, and they have shared experiences. Marketing people often visit the laboratories and manufacturing areas, and technical people frequently visit the marketplace.

Japanese technical and marketing people also socialize after hours. While this practice can be carried to excess, it's not uncommon for these people to go out after work to have a few beers together at a local bar, using such occasions to learn more about each other and to share ideas and information.

Because people know each other better, when it is time to form a multifunctional team for a new product development project, it is easier to contact the right people and to begin the project with little delay.

Providing Special Training

Another way of bridging the gap between marketing and technical people is to provide training programs that would teach each group something about each other's field. Technical people could be taught about market research techniques and the identification of marketplace needs and trends. Marketing people could be taught something about the technologies involved and the manufacturing methods for the company's products. Both groups could receive training in the preparation of business plans for major project proposals.

12 Stages of the New Product Development Cycle: Critical Issues in Project Management

THE THREE STAGES OF A NEW PRODUCT DEVELOPMENT PROJECT

Fast parallel development projects move along in an orderly series of steps. There are three distinct stages in a new product development project:

1. Preparation,
2. Performing the project,
3. Ending the project.

During each stage, a number of activities take place.

The Preparation Stage

This stage begins with developing an understanding of the needs of the marketplace. It moves on to the generating of ideas for products that satisfy those needs, it continues with the evaluation of a concept, and it ends with the determination of the feasibility of the idea, often a laboratory effort.

The multifunctional development team should be in place soon after the concept is evaluated and found to be acceptable. The desired product features and benefits should be frozen soon thereafter.

The Project Stage

This stage starts with the development of early prototypes. It then moves into later prototyping and sets the stage for preproduction testing and final production. It ends with release of the product into the marketplace.

The product design specifications should be frozen by the time the early prototypes are completed and before hard tooling is ordered.

The End Stage

This stage contains activities that bring the project to an orderly close, and it sets the stage for ongoing feedback and modification once the product is in the marketplace.

QUESTIONS TO ASK AT EACH STAGE

There are a number of questions that should be addressed at each step along the way. A suggested checklist of these questions follows:

Guide to New Product Development Checklist

The Preparation Stage

Identifying Marketplace Needs

Identifying and defining the marketplace needs, consistent with the company's capabilities, mission, and strategic plan.

Questions

What is the company's business and its market?

What is the company's mission and strategic plan?

Has the strategic plan been updated and communicated to the entire organization?

What are the company's marketing capabilities?

What are the company's technological capabilities?

Who are the company's lead customers?

Are company people visiting the lead customers?

What are the needs of the lead customers?

Do the lead customers have specific problems that the company can solve?

What are the industry trends?

What are the marketplace trends?

Idea Generation

Generating creative ideas that satisfy a marketplace need and identifying a specific concept for further evaluation.

Questions

Where are the ideas coming from?

How are ideas to be evaluated?

Who will evaluate the ideas?

What are the criteria to be used in evaluating ideas?

How are the ideas to be prioritized for further evaluation?

Have earlier ideas been reexamined?

Is guided brainstorming used to generate ideas?

Concept Evaluation

Testing the concept to see if it makes technological, marketing, financial, and business sense.

Questions

Does the idea fit the company's criteria for new products?

What are the new product's preliminary features and benefits?

Does the concept meet a marketplace need?

How big is the market for the proposed product?

Can a marketplace niche be dominated?

Is the proposed solution acceptable to potential customers?

Is anyone else addressing this marketplace need?

What are our competitors doing in this niche?

What will the competitor's reaction be?

Is the market local, national, or international?

Do we have the necessary marketing skills in place?

Do we have a channel to the marketplace? If not, can we develop it?

Will the new product cannibalize current product sales?

What advantage does the new product provide the customer?

What are the product cost objectives?

Is the technology available?

What are the elements of a development program?

What are the major technical problems that have to be solved?

What investment will be required for a development program?

Can there be a proprietary position?

Is patent coverage possible?

What is the probability of success?

What are the potential downside risks of proceeding?

What are the risks of not proceeding?

Feasibility

> Determining whether the concept is technologically possible, whether it can be manufactured at an acceptable cost and within a reasonable time frame, and whether there is a sufficient market potential to justify continuing on with the development project.

Questions

Have product features been frozen?

Is there a market for the product?

How big is the market?

What is the potential product's sales growth curve?

Who are the lead customers? Have they been involved?

What are the preliminary product specifications?

Has a multifunctional project team been formed?

Has the team selected its leader?

Has the team identified the project objectives?

Is there a product champion?

What are the potential production problems? Can they be overcome?

How long will it take to develop the product and what resources will be required?

How will the project be financed?

Has a business plan been prepared?

What is the potential return on the investment?

What is the potential for patent protection?

Has a patent search been done?

Has critical path project management been started?

Has a project cost tracking system been set up?

The Project Stage

Early Development

Developing early prototypes to test whether technical and production problems can be solved, to have something to show to the marketplace, and to prepare preliminary design specifications.

Questions

Does the marketplace need still exist?

How big is the market and how much can be captured?

Will a marketing program be supported after introduction?

Should the market and/or product development work be done with a joint venture partner?

Do we have the necessary marketing and sales skills in place?

What will be the competitors' reaction?

Has a name been selected for the product?

Has a channel to the marketplace been developed?

How will the product be positioned in the marketplace?

Have the barriers to entry been formulated?

What will the prototype look like?

What are the product performance specifications?

Can prototyping be accelerated?

What are the preliminary design specifications?

Do we have enough skills to make the product?

Do the process capabilities match the product requirements?

Does any major production equipment or tooling have to be ordered?

What is the delivery schedule?

What will be the cost?

Will manufacturing of this new product cause any environmental problems? Can they be overcome?

Have simulated use conditions been established?

Has patent coverage been sought?

Later Development

Developing final prototypes and placing the prototype at field test sites for evaluation.

Questions

Have design specifications been frozen?

Where are the field test sites and are the target companies willing to test the prototype?

Does the prototype satisfy the marketplace need?

Do the lead customers still like the idea?

What problems emerge from the test sites?

Has a marketing program been prepared?

Has a sales forecast been prepared?

Has tooling been specified and ordered?

How should the product be packaged?

How much will the product sell for?

Can we make money selling the product? How much?

Has a warranty/service program been prepared?

Do we have the necessary marketing and sales skills in place?

Are new facilities needed?

What production problems will there be?

What are the final product performance specifications?

Have reliability, safety, and stability studies been completed?

Has Quality Assurance begun to prepare process control specifications?

Has tentative production scheduling been determined?

What is the manufacturing plan? Have the raw materials been specified and selected?

Will the manufacturing and/or the product comply with all applicable environmental regulations?

Has patent protection been arranged?

What is the product life-cycle cash flow forecast?

Preproduction

Scaling up onto plant equipment, debugging tooling, and machinery; finalizing production and assembly methods; testing preproduction product; confirming production costs; refining marketing forecasts; finalizing quality assurance procedures; and training production workers.

Questions

Have tooling and machinery been received and debugged?

What is the final pricing of the product?

Is there an adequate profit potential?

Will the customers pay for the product?

Does the early production version satisfy the marketplace need?

Will the marketing program be supported financially?

Have the name and packaging designs been finalized?

Can the production problems be overcome in time and at a reasonable cost?

Have final specification sheets been prepared?

Have final drawings been finished?

Is there a final bill of materials?

Have the raw materials been ordered?

What will it cost to make the product?

Has production scheduling been finalized?

Has worker training been defined and scheduled?

Have Quality Assurance procedures been finalized?

Will the manufacturing and/or the product comply with all applicable environmental regulations?

How will the product be shipped?

Commercialization

Beginning to ship to a number of customers and fine-tuning marketing forecasts, sales methods, and Quality Assurance procedures, and, later, full-scale manufacturing, inventorying, and shipping of the new product.

Questions

What are the finalized marketing and sales plans?

Are sales training programs in place?

Is there a customer feedback loop in place for rapid information on product acceptance and problems?

Have first full production runs met design/production specifications?

What improvements in production plans can be made?

Have backup materials and/or manufacturing systems been determined and/or implemented?

Has the business plan been revised?

Has the product life-cycle cash flow forecast been finalized? What possible follow-on products can we make?

The End Stage (Project End and Evaluation)

Dissolving the new product development team, evaluating the project's performance, collecting all relevant documents into one location, recommending ways of improving project performance.

Questions

Is the team kept in place until after the product has been in production and doing well?

What can be learned from the way the project was conducted?

What should be done differently the next time?

Were all the right people on the team?

Were product features and design specifications frozen early enough?

How could the development program have been accelerated?

Did the project come in within cost and time budget?

Has all relevant documentation been collected and put in a safe place?

QUESTIONS TO ASK AT ALL STAGES OF DEVELOPMENT

Is there continuing top management commitment?

Does the product still fit the company's strategy?

Does it still make sense to continue this project?

Is the development project meeting its milestones and staying within budget?

Does the marketplace need still exist?

What additional benefit does this product offer over existing products?

Can the product be made at a cost that will allow an acceptable return?

What possible follow-on products can be made?

Will customers have to or be willing to pay for it?

Will the company support the marketing activities required?

What can be done to speed up the development program?

Is there still a product champion?

FLOW CHART FOR THE PRODUCT DEVELOPMENT PROCESS

A flow chart that graphically illustrates the path taken by a typical development project within the company can be a useful tool to have. It serves as a reminder to those involved in product development that there is a preferred way of doing things, it indicates those areas where senior management approvals are necessary, and it shows where product features and design specifications should be frozen. Figure 12.1 is an example of a flow chart for a manufacturing company.

Figure 12.1 Manufacturing Company's Flow Chart

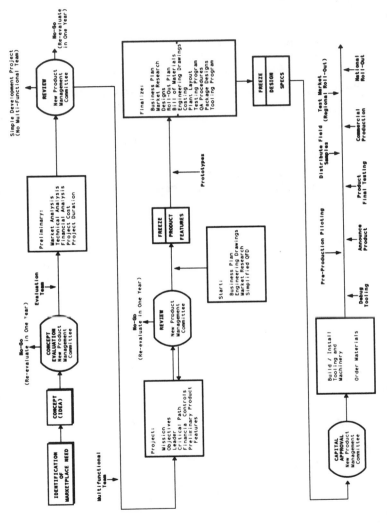

NEW PRODUCT DEVELOPMENT FLOWCHART

Forecasting and Controlling New Product

13 Development Costs

Development projects sometimes fail because their costs greatly exceed budget. Costs often seem to exceed budget because they were not estimated accurately in the first place.

The age-old dilemma is that it is extremely difficult to forecast new product development costs. But, to allocate scarce corporate funds intelligently, it is essential that a development project's anticipated cost and duration be estimated as early and as accurately as possible and that project costs be tracked and controlled.

WHY MISTAKES ARE MADE

It's human nature to want to present the most optimistic scenario possible. For this reason, marketing and sales people often overestimate new product sales and profits and technical people often underestimate development costs and duration.

Project costs are sometimes understated because technical people believe that they will not get management approval to go ahead with the project if it seems too expensive. Marketing and salespeople sometimes overestimate potential revenues from the new product because they have an overly optimistic view of the market-place.

Development people often resist making estimates in the first place because they think it ties their hands. They also believe they will have no opportunity to seek additional funds if a difficult technological problem emerges. As a result, they sometimes believe that they had better get extra money at the beginning of the project to cover such an eventuality.

Development people often don't have the right tools to help them estimate. Either they don't have the experience or knowledge to construct valid estimates, or they don't have access to software that will make it easier for them.

GUIDELINES FOR ESTIMATING PROJECT COSTS

The Experience Factor

There is no one good way to estimate costs. In the last analysis, an estimate is only as good as the experience and knowledge of the people doing the estimating. Good project cost estimating involves tapping into the wisdom of experts who, by painful trial and error over the years, have developed their own rules of thumb.

It's important that the leader and some of the people on the development team have had experience at project management and that they have a track record of accurately estimating project costs and duration. These people will have established their own rules on cost and resource allocating, knowing from experience what works and what does not.

Estimating as a Team Function

Project cost estimates done by only one person, no matter how experienced that person may be, often are inaccurate. One person cannot think of all the elements of a project, nor is one person able to anticipate all the things that may go wrong.

Project cost estimates are best done by members of a multi-functional team who work together to estimate the project's cost and duration. When all the key functions are represented, it's less likely that any critical milestones or tasks will be omitted from the estimate. As many as possible of the project's potential problems will be anticipated.

Elements of the Estimate

Good cost estimating takes into account the project's desired final results, the project's plan, and its achievement milestones. All the costs involved in new product development should be taken into account. For example, market introduction costs are often left out of the estimate. A grocery industry task force study[1] showed that 46% of new product roll-out costs went to advertising and promotion to convince customers to try the new product and 16% went to trade deals to get the retailers to out the new product into the stores. Only 18% of the development costs went to R&D and market research. If the new product development team had considered only the R&D and market research costs when estimating the project cost, they would have grossly underestimated the true cost of the project.

For large projects, a monthly cash flow projection is best, one which includes such costs as

- Manpower
- Supplies
- Laboratory equipment
- Prototype design and production
- Capital items (tooling and machinery)
- Contract engineering
- Roll-out sales costs
- Raw materials
- Market research
- Travel
- Patent and other legal fees
- Licensing fees
- Advertising, promotion, and training
- Preparation and publication of manuals

- Name research
- Customer focus groups
- Package and other design
- Outside consultants
- Shipping
- Miscellaneous expenses

Using Critical Path Software to Help Estimate Costs

Every development project is comprised of a series of tasks, each of which has a cost. Critical path management software can be used to help determine the project milestones, the tasks, and the subtasks that must be accomplished to achieve each milestone. Once the project has been broken up into its component tasks, it is much easier to estimate the costs involved.

EFFECT OF ACCELERATING THE PACE ON PROJECT COSTS

Not surprisingly, development costs rise dramatically when pressure is put on projects to accelerate the pace. Because it feared that the Japanese would capture the market, Xerox elected to step up the pace drastically when it was developing its 1045 copier.[2] Extra people and additional funds were added to the project when its timetable was advanced. Because of the rush, the product had moved into the pre-production stage before it was discovered that there was a major design flaw, one that would have been discovered earlier had the pace not been so rushed.

Xerox discovered that the wire harness that held the internal wires together was not designed properly and that it did not meet the company's quality standards. The harness had to be redesigned, and the project had to wait while that was accomplished. This mistake cost Xerox an extra $1 million.

This experience is not unusual. Projects can be speeded up drastically, but usually a very stiff price is paid, either because something falls between the cracks or because mistakes are made.

Under normal conditions, a development project has a natural pace. It takes time to do certain things. Innovative technology development takes a certain amount of time, no matter how much pressure there is to complete it. People need time to make the necessary connections in their minds and to be creative.

When development projects are accelerated beyond their natural pace, they become less efficient and their cost goes up dramatically. This is because there is a greater likelihood of mistakes being made. Each person added to the team contributes less, and each additional person has to go through has the same learning curve as did every other person on the project. Too many people get in each other's way.

Senior management must take great care when insisting on an earlier completion of a development project than originally planned. Sometimes, greatly accelerating the pace causes more harm than good. It's far better to insist on a fast pace at the beginning of the project, so that the team can plan its work and the resources needed accordingly.

FREEZING PRODUCT FEATURES AND DESIGN SPECIFICATIONS EARLY

Cost estimates are valid only if the product features and design specifications are frozen early, otherwise, all bets are off. Changing the product features and design specifications at a later date will only add to the costs of the project and cause unnecessary delay and confusion.

WHY IT'S BETTER TO ESTIMATE SLIGHTLY TOO LOW THAN TOO HIGH

One of Parkinson's Laws is that the amount of work to be performed will always increase to match the amount of resources available. This principle applies to development project management. If a project's estimated cost is set too high and its duration is too long, it's more than likely that the project will take too long and will cost too much.

It's better to estimate project costs slightly on the low side than to try to cover one's bets by estimating too high. If the estimate is slightly low, people will have a greater challenge than if it is too high.

If they have the right support and management commitment, chances are the development team will rise to the occasion and develop the product on schedule.

However, this is not intended as permission for senior management to cut every cost and duration estimate arbitrarily in half in the mistaken belief that it promotes faster product development. If unrealistic estimates are imposed on a development team that knows better, the project will likely fail.

AN INTERNAL BENCHMARKING APPROACH

Internal benchmarking uses past history as a guide to project estimating. To do this, the company keeps a record of every development project it has conducted, taking note of

- The nature of the project
- The project's key milestones
- The project's actual total cost and duration
- The project's estimated total cost and duration
- Who was on the development team
- Who was the team leader
- Who was responsible for the estimating

The internal benchmark provides a checklist and a set of guidelines that help future development teams to know whether their estimates deviate from the historical norm for a similar type of project.

ESTIMATING LOST OPPORTUNITY COSTS

Management usually concentrates on what it will cost to do a development project. While this is an important consideration, a better question might be: "What will it cost us if we don't do this development project?"

When estimating the cost of a major development project, it is useful to examine what it would cost the company if the project were not funded and if the new product were not developed. This is the cost of the opportunity that would be lost if a competitor had the idea for the new product and got to the marketplace before anyone else.

A lost opportunity analysis is a what-if scenario that is based on an understanding of the marketplace. Such an analysis considers the life cycle of the potential new product and its potential sales and profits minus the development and introduction costs on a net present value basis. It also considers the implications of someone else developing and controlling a new technology.

A decision not to fund a development project should be made only after the lost opportunity cost is known. Only then can decisions be made with a full understanding of the impact of that decision.

CONTROLLING PROJECT COSTS

Project cost control is essential. It involves cost estimating, tracking costs, project cash flow management, and managing fixed and variable costs. A cost control system gives up to the minute information on cost performance, identifies potential problems, and identifies the true cost of each milestone.

Project control tools must be able to measure the status of accomplishments, measure resources used, compare expenditures to projections, allow diagnosis and replanning, have a quick response to changing levels of expense, provide exception reporting, and evaluate alternative solutions.

Since no companies are alike and no projects are alike, all cost control systems are different, but they have certain similarities:

- They all start with a good projected budget that is based on critical path milestones and resource estimates.
- They use cost accounting systems.
- There are weekly time cards submitted for all projects.
- The system is computerized.
- Reports are submitted to the project manager on a regular basis.
- All expenditures can be traced readily.

It helps if there is a member of the accounting department on every project team from the start of the project and all times thereafter.

Endnotes

[1]"Pinning Down Costs of Product Introductions," *The Wall Street Journal,* November 26, 1990, p. B1.

[2]Graves, S. B., "Why Costs Increase When Projects Accelerate," *Research-Technology Management,* January-February, 1989, pp. 16-18.

14 Outside Sourcing of New Products and Designs

Every company ought to consider all its options for obtaining new products and not be totally locked into only developing products or designs internally. Sometimes, companies can do very well by licensing a new product or design from outside the company.

Just as there are advantages and problems with developing new products internally, there are advantages and disadvantages to outside sourcing of new products and designs.

ADVANTAGES OF OUTSIDE SOURCING

Rapid Entry into the Marketplace

Speed is of the essence in getting a new product to the marketplace. A product that is being sold successfully elsewhere has already gone through all the necessary stages of development, has had its start-up problems resolved, and has established its channels of distribution. Once it has been customized to meet your particular marketplace needs, such a product can be ready to go very quickly.

A New Look for the Customers

Customers are always looking for something new, whether it is a wholly new product, a change in design, or even a change in packaging. A new product or design from another country can provide a fresh look that might appeal to customers who are getting weary of products they have been looking at for years.

Sometimes, importing something that is a little unusual can revive a flagging market. Kellogg studied European muesli cereals that originally had been invented in Switzerland.[1] These cereals, which contained slightly sweetened and very crunchy fruit, nuts, and grains, were very different from the cereals that Kellogg had been selling in the United States. Kellogg introduced its own version, the Mueslix brand, and this turned out to be one of its most successful new product introductions. The new cereal was described as being healthy, natural, and slightly different, all of which enabled Kellogg to capture market share in an otherwise flat market.

Tested Customer Acceptance

A product that has been sold elsewhere has demonstrated some degree of customer acceptance, at least in its own country. While this is no guarantee that the same product will secure customer acceptance in your marketplace, it is at least evidence that customers *somewhere* tried the product and found it acceptable.

Procter & Gamble realized that West German environmentalists had a very strong following. In response, P&G developed a refillable laundry detergent package for that market. The product was received well. P&G then modified the package slightly and introduced it into test market in the United States as the Downy refillable detergent package.

Established Product Cost and Margins

One of the great uncertainties of new product development is whether the new product will meet the cost and gross margin guidelines required by the company. A product that is already made elsewhere has known costs and margins. At very least, this provides the licensee with a benchmark for manufacturing costs and margins.

Minimal Development Costs

When a product is licensed, all or nearly all of its development has been completed by someone else, at their expense. To be sure, there will be costs of introducing the product into your manufacturing, sales, and distribution system, but they will be far less than they would have been if you had been obliged to go through all the earlier stages of development.

Preestablished Manufacturing Procedures

One problem in any development program is the extensive learning curve in Manufacturing before a new product can be produced. With a licensed product that already has a manufacturing track record, the learning curve can be minimized greatly. The new product can move into manufacturing with a minimum of confusion.

Readily Available Tooling

Tooling can take a long time to obtain, fine-tune, and integrate into production. When a product is acquired from outside, the required tooling is obtained from the licensee. Most important, the tooling has been debugged previously by someone else.

DRAWBACKS AND RISKS

Outside sourcing of new products and designs is not always a good experience or always possible. While bad experiences are not commonplace occurrences, they sometimes make people wish they never tried to license a product from someone else.

Messy Legal Arrangements

Licensing a product requires a license agreement, a legal document that details the rights and obligations of both parties concerned, the licensor and the licensee. The agreements can end up containing so many clauses and take so long to be drawn up that the marketplace opportunity is lost. This is especially a problem with license agreements between U.S. and foreign companies, where lawyers from both countries are involved in the transaction and where different languages are spoken.

Greedy Licensors

Many licensing arrangements fall apart because the licensor is too greedy. A potential licensee will sometimes identify a candidate product that will fit a particular marketplace need, only to find that the licensor's financial demands make it impossible to obtain a reasonable profit margin.

Incompatibility with Local Customs

Great care must be taken to make sure that the potential new product is compatible with local customers. Kellogg Company licensed a liquid yogurt drink from Europe, and when it tried to introduce it into the United States, it had very poor results. As it turned out, Americans were not ready for Kellogg's LeShake yogurt drink, and it failed to grab hold. This was a surprise to Kellogg because the drink was so popular in Europe.

When importing or exporting a new product, care must be taken with the name. When Chevrolet exported its Nova automobile into South America, anticipated sales never materialized. Chevrolet was upset when it discovered that the word Nova sounded like the Spanish words *no va*, which mean "won't go" in that language. Coca-Cola was disappointed when it tried to introduce Coca-Cola in China. As it turned out, the name sounded like Chinese words that meant "dead rat" in one dialect and "bitter" in another.

Grossly Inflated Claims

The licensor wants to sell the potential licensee his or her product and will do everything possible to make it sound attractive. Sometimes, the claims will be grossly exaggerated. Unless great care is taken to confirm that the claims are as represented, the licensee can be fooled. The potential licensee wants to believe the claims and will often be incredibly gullible. The old adage still applies: "If something sounds too good to be true, it probably is."

Lack of Acceptance Within the Company

A licensed product will sometimes fail to be launched because the people within the licensee's company fail to support it. They have the "not invented here" syndrome and will resist the introduction of the new product because they didn't think of it themselves. They drag their heels and, if enough time passes, the marketplace opportunity is lost.

Lack of a Marketplace Need

A product that satisfies a need in one country may not be appropriate anywhere else. Adequate market research is necessary to confirm that there really is a market need for the new product.

GETTING STARTED

To improve the odds of success when seeking products from overseas, look for a product that already has a fairly broad customer base in its country of origin. This way, you will at least know that the product has marketplace acceptance somewhere. For example, U.S. breweries waited until Sapporo Breweries in Japan had demonstrated that there was a substantial market for a new "dry" beer before starting to make their own versions of the product. Dry beers have since become a successful market entry in the United States.

A larger U.S. company is likely to find overseas products that it can license by asking its foreign affiliates or divisions to look for such opportunities. Information on appropriate and available products is more readily accessible to those people who are on the scene, especially those who know their parent company's needs and its marketplace.

There also are experienced consultants who link up potential product opportunities with licensees. This can work well, provided the consultant is given enough information about your company's needs and its marketplace niche.

INTERNAL VERSUS EXTERNAL PRODUCT DEVELOPMENT: THE PROPER BALANCE

Licensing a new product from someone else is not appropriate for everyone. Under the right circumstances, it is a way of getting new products to the marketplace faster and being more responsive to marketplace needs. A company should never stop developing new products internally and should concentrate most of its efforts in that direction. However, because there is a chance that licensing a tested product from elsewhere has the potential of speeding up the process, it pays to keep an open mind about looking for new products outside the company

Endnote

[1]McCarthy, M. J. "U.S. Companies Shop Abroad for Product Ideas," *The Wall Street Journal*, March 14, 1990, p. 1.

15 Using Business Plans for Major Projects

A good business plan is as much an essential component of new product development programming as anything else. Often, the existence of a business plan makes the difference between project success or failure.

Many people hate to prepare business plans. They don't understand them, they feel intimidated by them, and they believe a business plan locks them into a program from which there is no escape. It's important to overcome this negative bias and to begin to use business plans for major projects.

Business plans impose a disciplined approach to projects and provide milestones for measuring progress once they have started. A good business plan is strongly skewed toward information about the marketplace. Having a plan makes it more likely that when a major project is started, it will address a real marketplace need.

A business plan is a written representation of a proposal for a business venture, whether the proposal is for a new product or for an entirely new business. It serves a number of useful purposes:

- It crystallizes and focuses ideas and eliminates shallow thinking.
- It helps determine whether a project is worth doing.

155

- It creates a path for management to follow during the stages of a project.
- It provides a plan around which a development team can rally.
- It considers possible risks and addresses ways of dealing with them.
- It creates benchmarks for measuring progress.
- It is a persuasive way of convincing someone that it's a good idea to fund a project.

Business plans are not designed to stifle the entrepreneurial spirit; rather, they are used to provide a framework to be used to enlist the approval, aid, and support of others within the organization and to provide a checklist of important issues that should be addressed.

CONTENTS OF A BASIC BUSINESS PLAN

The following business plan outline should not to be taken literally. It is to be used as a checklist of items that ought to be considered for incorporation into the plan. The plan preparer is encouraged to use judgment.

1. Table of Contents
2. Executive Summary (The Executive Summary provides a concise overview of the entire business plan.)
3. The Business Concept (This section sets the stage for the proposed project or product by positioning it within the context of the company's business.)
   a. description of the company's business
   b. the company's criteria for new products
   c. brief description of the product and its current position on the new product development cycle
   d. description of how the proposed product will satisfy a need in the marketplace
   e. how the proposed product will contribute to the business
4. Market Analysis (This section describes whatever is known about the marketplace niche into which the new product will fit and positions the new product within that niche.)

    a. industry description and outlook

    b. detailed description of the marketplace need

    c. historical growth rates of target markets

    d. description and location of the marketplace niche

    e. potential for domination of the niche

    f. potential market share

    g. distribution channels and seasonality

    h. contacts with potential lead customers

    i. how similar products are purchased and by whom

    j. minimum functional performance characteristics for the new product (from the user's perspective)

    k. critical regulatory requirements

    l. pricing requirements of the marketplace

5. Competition (An emerging new product is likely to face competition from more mature organizations with greater resources. This section seeks to identify potential competitors and their strengths, weaknesses, and market share. It also describes barriers by which the competition will try to block entry of the new product.)

    a. identification

    b. strengths and weaknesses

    c. market share

    d. barriers to entry into the market

6. Description of the Proposed Product (This section is used to define precisely what is intended to be developed and marketed.)

    a. detailed product description and features

    b. description of the marketplace need that will be met by the product

    c. specific user benefits and advantages of the product

    d. product life cycle after commercialization

    e. production cost objectives

7. Product Development Plans (Product development plans are necessary to make certain that a product that meets marketplace

needs is developed and delivered to the marketplace in as short a time as possible.)

   a. resources required (manpower, materials, tooling, and capital equipment)

   b. details of the development program

   c. makeup of the development team

   d. critical path chart (with milestones)

   e. new technology required for the development program

   f. plans to relate to lead customers

   g. joint development partner(s), if any are planned

   h. how quality functional deployment (QFD) groups will be used to define design specifications and product features

   i. when product design specifications and product features will be frozen

   j. the name of the product champion

8. Marketing, Sales, and Distribution Plans (This section defines strategy and charts the marketing direction for the product.)

   a. market penetration strategy

   b. distribution channels

   c. sales strategy

   d. pricing

   e. service and warranty policies

   f. advertising, public relations, and promotion

   g. plans to acquire feedback from the end users

   h. future marketing and sales strategies

   i. rewards for the sales force

9. Manufacturing and Quality Assurance Plans (Efficient manufacturing start-up and production are major factors in a product's success. This section defines plans for manufacturing and controlling the quality of the new product.)

   a. nature and extent of production facilities required

   b. current production capacity (internal and external)

   c. additional production capacity required

    d. implementation schedule for manufacturing

    e. additional manufacturing equipment required

    f. identification of suppliers

    g. detailed quality assurance plans

10. New Business Management Team (The management team is a very important consideration during the evaluation of a proposed new business venture.)

    a. key personnel

    b. planned additions to management

11. Anticipated Proprietary Position(s) (This section is used to describe a means by which the competition is to be kept out of the marketplace as long as possible, whether by patent protection, trade secrecy, or other means.)

12. Risk Factors and Analysis (Risks are an anticipated element of any new venture. This section analyzes the risks inherent in the project and offers suggestions for dealing with these risks.)

13. Financial Analyses (This section is a financial representation of all the information presented in the other sections of the plan.) Project cost estimates should include expenses associated with

    a. manpower

    b. equipment and materials

    c. manufacturing trials

    d. consulting

    e. prototypes

    f. outside development

    g. software purchase and development

    h. market research

    i. on-line data retrieval

    j. market introduction costs

As the project goes on and it is possible to forecast, with greater accuracy, the potential revenues and earnings of the product once it is in the marketplace, five-year projected cash flow and income statements should be prepared.

Cash flow analyses and income statements should be shown

monthly until the breakeven point is reached and quarterly there-after.

Projected needs for major capital tooling and other equipment and machinery should also be indicated.

14. Pulling It All Together (This section provides, in summary form, an overview of the entire development project, using a computer-driven critical path chart.)

    a. critical path chart of all activities

    b. list of key milestones and target dates

    c. overall cost targets

15. Funds Needed and Use of Funds (This section uses information developed in the financial analysis to indicate how much money is needed to take the project through to completion.)

16. Proposed Method of Financing the Project (When appropriate, this section can be used to propose various means by which the project can be financed.)

17. Business Plan Appendix

    a. financial analyses

    b. market research reports

    c. pertinent published information

    d. relevant patents

    e. significant contracts

    f. photographs or drawings of the new product

    g. other material in support of the project

    h. critical path chart

THE BUSINESS PLAN IN RELATION TO THE STAGES OF THE NEW PRODUCT DEVELOPMENT CYCLE

Plans should start out as fairly simple documents. Later, they should be revised and made more complex as the project progresses and more information is known.

When prepared at an early stage of the product development cycle, the business plan serves as a relatively simple project proposal. It will contain less information than a plan prepared at a later stage. A plan for a major project is not necessary until after a project has passed the concept evaluation stage.

GUIDELINES FOR THE PREPARATION OF A BUSINESS PLAN

1. The business plan should be as short as is reasonably possible, preferably containing no more than 25 to 30 pages of text plus financial data and other support material.
2. It is best to start with the marketing section, then do the product and manufacturing sections, and finish the remaining sections of the plan. The Executive Summary, not to exceed two pages, should be done last.
3. The plan doesn't need to be very fancy; use graphs, charts, and other visual aids where possible to enhance the presentation.
4. Use a typewritten $8\frac{1}{2} \times 11$" format and use a loose-leaf binder to facilitate future revisions.
5. Make sure that a team prepares the plan and that the team seeks comments from individuals unrelated to the project as the plan is being written.
6. The plan should be updated every time a significant project milestone or another stage in the development cycle has been reached.
7. Because of the amount of work involved in its preparation, a business plan should be prepared only for major projects.

Business plans are an essential aspect of product development. Without a good business plan for a major new product, neither senior management nor the project team will really understand the reason for a project's existence or the path by which it will be accomplished. People need to overcome their reluctance to develop good business plans and begin to view them as an important aspect of their business life.

16 New Product Development in the Skunk Works

THE HISTORY OF THE SKUNK WORKS

A skunk works is an area of the company that is set aside and wholly dedicated to a specific new product development project. The term comes from Al Capp's "Li'l Abner" comic strip where "skunk works" was the name given to the "Kickapoo Joy Juice Brewery."

A skunk works operation is isolated from the rest of the company and it is not subject to any of the bureaucratic procedures that prevail elsewhere in the company. The idea is that isolating the facility and minimizing the paperwork will make it easier for a development team to get its work done.

Because the skunk works teams typically are comprised of scientists and engineers, they generally are used to develop concepts and early prototypes that use an advanced technology. Later stages of the development project, such as final engineering, manufacturing, and marketing of the product need the skills of other people within the company.

The original industrial skunk works was established by Clarence L. "Kelly" Johnson at Lockheed in 1943.[1] Johnson took a team of 120 engineers into a tent that had rudimentary furniture and equipment and worked with them to develop a jet fighter that could fly faster than 500 mph. It took the team just 43 days to design the entire airplane, a spectacular performance.

Later, Lockheed used the same skunk works approach to develop the SR-71 and the U-2 planes. Lockheed's skunk works later was renamed officially the Advanced Development Projects Organization.

Since then, many companies have attempted to re-create the skunk works for crash development programs. While most skunk works projects have failed to deliver, there have been some notable successes.

Xerox developed prototypes for its Model 2510 copier and two other machines in a skunk works area. The group of 26 engineers was totally isolated from the rest of the company.

Ultra Technologies was founded in 1984 as a wholly owned subsidiary of Eastman Kodak. It started out in a skunk works, totally separated from the rest of the company in an empty seminary building in Rochester, New York, a space that could hardly be described as a being a comfortable place to work. Lithium batteries with long life were developed in the skunk works, and these became the basis of Kodak's entry into the consumer battery business.

THE FUNDAMENTAL PROBLEM WITH THE SKUNK WORKS

Consistently fast and high-quality new product development is a multi-functional task, especially if it is to be responsive to marketplace needs. It requires the involvement of all the departments within a company, not just a group of scientists and engineers set apart by themselves. A skunk works can take a development project just so far and no farther.

If not all the necessary skills are represented on the team, the skunk works can develop products that are hard or impossible to make, that may not meet marketplace needs, and that are too costly.

The success of a good skunk works operation depends totally on the project leader. In industry, there are few "Kelly" Johnsons who are capable of inspiring a team of isolated engineers to greatness. Further, senior managers tend to meddle with the skunk works operation. There are not too many of them who are able to believe that a wholly independent development group can be trusted.

A skunk works operation can siphon good people away from

other development projects where their skills could be put to good use. These people become unavailable to help others within the company, and, in so doing, the rest of the company slows down.

Being a member of a skunk works can be an extremely stressful experience, especially if the project is unsuccessful. It is very demotivating for the entire team when projects fail to deliver. Team members who have had the experience are not likely to want to work on other development teams in the future.

Further, skunk works team members often are by passed when opportunities for promotion or advancement come up. They are out of sight and, often, out of mind.

WHEN A SKUNK WORKS APPROACH MIGHT BE APPROPRIATE

Although it is rarely appropriate to set up a skunk works operation, there are a few instances where it might work.

A skunk works might be used to accomplish a small but critical portion of a major development project, for example, when some of the team members need to maintain an intense effort for a short period of time. To be effective, the skunk works effort must be within the context of a multifunctional team approach in which the skunk works team leader reports to the overall team leader.

If there is an extreme need for secrecy during the development of a highly technical project, a skunk works can be a useful way of achieving that goal. It should be remembered, though, that this can backfire. When there are rigidly imposed conditions of secrecy, it might be hard to get important information that is necessary for the project *into* the skunk works.

STAFFING THE SKUNK WORKS

People are best suited to working in a skunk works if they are self-starting and self-directed individualists. Typically, people who do well in a skunk works have had plenty of development experience with little benefit of any formal training. They tend to be practical engineers who have little tolerance for bureaucratic nonsense or for anyone who gets in their way.

Ideally, the skunk works leader should have all the attributes of a "Kelly" Johnson. The leader should be trusted by senior management, know how to make things happen with a minimum of fuss, and know how to lead a group of independent and unconstrained people who love to beat the bureaucracy.

GUIDELINES FOR OPERATING A SKUNK WORKS

There are some guidelines that can be observed if a skunk works is to be established:

1. Isolate the skunk works as far away from the company mainstream as is possible but not so far away that it is difficult for it to pull in additional resources when needed.
2. Make sure the skunk works leader has the complete support of senior management. Have the leader report to someone at highest level possible.
3. Minimize the size of the group. A large group defeats the purpose of the skunk works.
4. Minimize report writing requirements and leave the team alone so long as it is meeting its preestablished and agreed-upon milestones.
5. Dedicate people to only one project at a time.
6. Don't stint on development funds.
7. Make sure the skunk works team keeps in close contact with its internal or external customers.

OVERALL CONSIDERATION

Unless there are special and compelling reasons, a skunk works approach to new product development is not a good idea. Skunk works projects rarely go as well as hoped and when they fail they leave a trail of bad feelings and shattered dreams. In addition, no matter how well they work, they rarely involve all the key functional areas within the company. As a result, people who were not in the skunk works project have learned little about how to conduct a good development project.

Endnote

[1]Wolff, M. F. "To Innovate Faster, Try the Skunk Works," *Research-Technology Management,* September-October, 1987, pp. 72-73.

17 Killing a Development Project

There is a point of diminishing return past which it doesn't pay to pour any more money or energy into a project. Knowing when it is time to pull the plug and actually doing it are critical to any company that is conducting new product development.

All too often, company management allows nonperforming projects to go on year after year, continuing to fund them with no apparent end in sight. This is an unhealthy and passive approach to project management, and it is debilitating for the company and its people. Money spent on a project that is going nowhere takes money out of the cash pool that could be used to fund more worthwhile projects.

WHEN TO DO A MAJOR PROJECT EVALUATION

It's time for an appraisal of a major development project when there seems to be no end to the cash drain and when its outcome seems uncertain.

A major project evaluation is appropriate when

- A project seems to be costing too much and taking too long
- When the marketplace seems to be changing

- When senior management is feeling weary of the project
- When the development team is doubtful of the project's outcome

A major project evaluation helps company management make informed decisions about the wisdom of continuing to invest in a major development project, and it helps people learn from their mistakes. An evaluation is of value, whether or not it ends up recommending that a project be terminated. Much is learned in the process that will help the development team speed up the project if a decision is made to continue it.

ELEMENTS OF A PROJECT EVALUATION

A project evaluation measures the degree of interest in a project, the extent to which there is still a market for the product, and the likelihood that the development team will meet its milestones.

The evaluation examines how the project got where it is, what its problems are, what its cash situation is, where it seems to be going, how people feel about it, and what needs to be done to get it back on track. It asks the following specific questions:

- Is there still senior management support for the project?
- Is there still a dedicated product champion?
- Has the team leader been a good project manager?
- Does the marketplace need still exist?
- Is the technology required to complete the project readily available and well understood?
- Are there other, more meaningful projects that are competing for the same resources?
- Are all the team members still feeling a sense of urgency about the project, and do they want to stay with it?
- Are project cost projections still realistic, and are they being met?
- Does the product still fit the company's business?
- Exactly how far along is each major element of the project?

- Have product features and design specifications been frozen early?
- Has there been a multifunctional team in place since the beginning of the project? Have key suppliers and customers been involved?
- What is the market potential of the new product and what are the marketing and sales strategies?
- Is the technology unique and can there be a proprietary position?
- Do potential customers exist? Would the new product offer them a distinct advantage?
- Are lead customers still interested in the project?
- How good has the development team and leadership performance been?
- Is there a clear identification of project milestones and what are they?
- Have the project milestones been met regularly?
- Can there be a proprietary position for the product?
- What are the needs for further development?
- Is there a problem with the availability of necessary raw materials?
- Who are the potential competitors and what is their reaction likely to be?
- How much money has been spent on the project and what additional funding will be needed to finish it?
- What are the risks of continuing the project? Of not continuing it?
- What are the capital equipment, tooling, and space needs?
- Is there a good business plan for the project?
- Are there potential legal and environmental problems that will have to be addressed?

WHO DOES THE EVALUATION?

The project evaluation is best done by outsiders, people from elsewhere within the company or external consultants. These are people who have no vested interest in whether or not the project is continued. If done by internal people, the evaluation is best done by a team made up of people from Marketing, R&D, Engineering, Manufacturing, and Finance. The evaluators should have a good track record of new product development themselves and a deep understanding of the important issues. It's also very important that the evaluators be trusted both by senior management and by the project team members.

KILLING THE PROJECT

After a project has been in development for a while, it's not unusual to find that the original estimates have been too optimistic or that it may be too difficult or too expensive to develop the necessary technology. There may be other signs that indicate that, if pursued further, the project is destined to be a failure or to achieve only marginal success.

It's time to kill the project when it is apparent that it will take too long and cost too much to finish the project or if the developed product won't work. A project should be killed when reasonable milestones can't be met, when the team feels it's hopeless, when the product won't meet a marketplace need, if customers are no longer interested, or if the product will be too late to matter.

Willingness to kill a project requires a management belief that all development projects are sunk costs, at least until a project is completed and the new product is making money. Without this attitude firmly established, development projects will drift on year after year, in the hopes that they will someday succeed.

It takes guts to kill an expensive major project, especially one that has been going on for a long time. It's also hard to kill a project if its champion has a high position in the company.

If a company is taking on a wide range of projects and is taking enough risk, there are bound to be some projects that don't make the grade. If a company's management has a healthy attitude about risk and a willingness to tolerate failure, it will understand that killing poor projects is just another aspect of good project management.

It's no shame to kill a project that ought to be ended. In fact, the members of a project team sometimes are just begging someone to end their misery. They feel relief when it's all over. It's less hard to pick up the pieces than people think, especially if people are allowed to go on to another project. Team members stop feeling pain, and management has important resources freed up for something else.

Keep in mind, though, that a killed project should be looked at a year later to see if changing conditions make it more attractive at that time. More favorable marketplace trends, better technology, and more resources may combine to warrant a fresh look at the shelved project.

18 Encouraging Creativity and Innovation

Creativity is an unpredictable, vague, and somewhat obscure process. It results in an idea for a new product or a new way of doing something that is original, new, and significant. It is an intuitive way in which a person rearranges vague ideas and observations and constructs a new reality or a new way of looking at things. The creative thought is usually a surprise, although, after a little more reflection, the new idea seems so obvious that the person wonders why it hadn't been thought of before by someone else.

In the mid-1950s, Malcolm McLean created the concept of containerized shipping, an idea that later became the basis of the Sea-Land Company, the first shipping company to ship goods in containers. The breakthrough idea came when McLean realized that it made little sense to pack objects into crates and later to unload the crates from a truck at dockside prior to putting them aboard a ship. He reasoned that it would be far easier if the entire truck container were put on the ship. There would be less breakage and less theft and the handling costs would be lower.

McLean's thinking was very creative. It enabled his company to take off and prosper. This sort of creativity is necessary for any company that wants to experience significant growth from its new product development activities, especially if it intends to accomplish anything other than develop "me too" products.

To succeed in the marketplace, new products have to meet a marketplace need, and they have to meet that need creatively. For this to happen, a company has to understand the nature of creativity and innovation and has to establish an environment that will make it more likely that they will occur.

STAGES IN THE CREATIVE PROCESS

There is always a moment when the creative insight is realized, and it seems as if it just happened by itself all at once. In reality, creativity is a sequential process that takes place in a series of steps. According to Badawy, these stages are[1]

1. Identification of the problem
2. Gathering of information
3. Incubation
4. Insight
5. Validation

Identification of the Problem

The creative process begins when a person realizes that there is a problem that needs to be solved. This realization sets in motion a process of thinking, wondering, contemplating, and otherwise gnawing on the problem in an effort to find an acceptable solution. Creative people welcome problems as an opportunity to engage in a process that, while it may be frustrating and confusing at times, is stimulating, engaging, and sometimes rewarding.

Gathering of Information

At this stage, the creative person is gathering as much information as possible about the problem. The person is collecting ideas and information, is talking to many people, and is building a base of knowledge, not all of which is entirely relevant. This is the time to learn, and it often takes the form of literature searches and laboratory experimentation. At some point, the person realizes that this stage has gone on long enough, that the gathering of any more information would probably be overkill.

Incubation

This stage goes on in the creative person's subconscious mind. It is not possible to hurry the process along by a force of will or by any other means. Creativity will happen when it is time and there is no way of predicting when it will take place. It is certain that there needs to be a period of incubation while the person's brain sifts all the possibilities, without any awareness by the person that this is going on.

The incubation period appears to work best when the person is doing something else, and often there have to be some periods of sleep involved. For example, Kekule, a great chemist of the last century, dreamed about a snake that was eating its own tail. When he awakened, he realized that he had visualized the structure of the benzene molecule, six carbon atoms held together in a ring structure.

The fact that the period of incubation cannot be rushed can be very frustrating to the creative person, especially if there is a deadline to be met. Unfortunately, putting pressure on a person to hurry up is a sure way of delaying the appearance of the creative insight.

Insight

Insight is that stunning moment when the solution to the problem is realized, as if the lights were suddenly turned on in a very dark room. Insight usually occurs while doing something totally unrelated to the original problem, often while doing something that is relaxing or while thinking about something totally unrelated.

Many people say that they have their most creative insights while shaving, while showering, when exercising, just before awakening in the morning, while driving a car, and at other times totally unrelated to their work environment.

Validation

This is the hard part of the creative process, the tedious stage when the idea must be tested to make sure it is valid with respect to its newness, its manufacturability, its ability to meet a marketplace need, its cost, and its reliability. Many ideas that appeared to be creative and new fall apart at this stage, much to the mortification and discomfort of the person who had the creative idea in the first place.

CATEGORIES OF INNOVATION

Product innovation can be classified in a number of ways, according to the perceptions of the manufacturing company and the ultimate users of the products. A company needs to decide the mix of innovation categories that best satisfies its strategic plan for growth and should certainly not concentrate on only one form of innovation. According to Gobeli and Brown, there are four types of innovations:[2]

1. Incremental product innovations
2. Application innovations
3. Technical innovations
4. Radical innovations

Incremental Product Innovations

Incremental product innovations are improvements in a product line that already exists. As such, they rarely offer opportunity for major growth for the company. Such products are sold into the same market as were the original products. Annual model changes and "new and improved" soap powders and detergents are examples of this type of innovation. They require little technological input and little customer training. Most innovations in American industry are in this category. In many cases, this is all a company does with its new product development activities.

Application Innovations

With application innovations, products already in existence are either left as is or are modified slightly to satisfy a previously unmet customer need in a marketplace niche that is new to the company. The application of currently existing technology is used to develop these products. The breakthroughs are marketing, not engineering or scientific. Because they require market research to identify new opportunities, they are not as common as they should be. Companies often are reluctant to conduct the market research, and there may not be a good bridge between the marketing and the technical people.

Technical Innovations

These are scientific and engineering innovations that often are invisible to the customer although they are exciting to the innovators. While such innovations may be new to the company, they offer few new benefits to the buyers, and, unless there is an enormous commitment to customer education, the product will go nowhere.

Sometimes these are products in search of a marketplace. They are not usually of great value to the company, unless it has deep pockets, is willing to commit substantial resources, and has plenty of patience and luck. Even then, if the customers cannot be convinced that the new product will do something for them at a price they are willing to pay, the company will not benefit from the technological breakthrough.

Radical Innovations

Actually, very few product introductions are really new to the company and its customers. They rarely happen and they rarely are the basis of new industries. When very significant innovations happen, whole new companies are formed and the industry is revolutionized. Radical innovations involve entirely new technology, they capture the customer's imagination, and they provide them with real benefits that require little selling.

There are many examples of radical innovations. Some of these are the personal computer, the fax machine, CAD equipment, television, telephones, Kleenex tissues, instant coffee, condensed soups, frozen vegetables, airplanes, birth control pills, automobiles, xerography, and penicillin. All these innovations were truly new to the world, and each of them was the basis of an entirely new industry.

It is widely believed that radical innovations are most likely to come from outside the company, but this is not always the case. For example, Pratt & Whitney and Rolls Royce converted from the piston to the jet engine without resorting to outside help. Nylon was invented at DuPont, the company that originally developed rayon, a very different synthetic fiber. Two carriage makers, Durant and Fisher Body, responded to the competitive challenge of the marketplace by learning how to make automobiles. Durant later became General Motors and Fisher Body became a significant car body manufacturer.

CHARACTERISTICS OF CREATIVE INDIVIDUALS

It's not possible to predict whether a person will be creative under any particular circumstances. Creativity is something that is known after the fact. Just as people have varying degrees of intelligence or height or weight, they possess varying degrees of creativity. Everyone is creative to some degree, although some people are more creative than others.

There is little evidence to support the belief that there is any particular relationship between creativity and intelligence. In fact, intelligence is by no means a predictor of creativity.

Intelligence is very different from creativity. Intelligence is a predictable ability to store and process information in a linear manner and to come out with the solution to a problem quickly and accurately. Creativity, on the other hand, depends on the mind's ability to range over a broad area and come up with the unpredictable. Creativity is a divergent process, and there is no knowing in advance what sort of idea will emerge.

When viewed as a group, on average, very creative people seem to share some attributes in common. Very creative people

- Are often nonconformists
- Don't like bureaucracies
- Don't think on demand
- Tend to be self-stimulating and self-directed
- Tend to be more imaginative than most people
- Are often fiercely independent
- Are especially observant
- Have plenty of energy

Creative people tend to be more interested in what is going on, and they have a greater need to be given detailed reasons why they are asked to do something. They are likely to be turned off if they find themselves in an environment where their opinions and feelings are not taken seriously.

CHARACTERISTICS OF CREATIVE COMPANIES

Some companies have much more creative environments than do others. These companies have some or all of the following characteristics in common:

- They have a strategic plan for new product development, and everyone in the company is familiar with the plan.

- They keep close tabs on the marketplace, monitoring performance of their new products, and they are willing to learn from their mistakes.

- They tolerate failures and encourage risk taking.

- They encourage wide-open communication, and they minimize bureaucratic procedures.

- They encourage experimentation with new ideas.

- They recognize that people need stimulus from outside sources.

- They maintain a sense of humor and don't run the organization too rigidly.

- They promote participative decision making at the lowest level possible.

- They encourage travel and attendance at trade shows and professional meetings.

- They reward failures by concentrating on what has been learned in the process of conducting the project that failed.

- They know that it is important to prioritize projects and to eliminate or postpone those that are no longer worthy of support.

- They have realistic but firm deadlines for their development projects.

- They listen to ideas from people at all levels of the company.

- They understand that a high level of creativity and innovation encourages high morale, not the other way around.

- They do everything possible to minimize anxiety levels within the company because they know that anxious people won't be creative or energetic.

PROMOTING CREATIVITY AND INNOVATION

It's impossible to schedule the creative or innovative thought. All the company leadership can do is to establish an environment where creativity and innovation are encouraged. The leadership should not get in the way of creative people and should reward them at every opportunity.

Some guidelines for establishing an environment that is friendly to creativity and innovation are

1. Widely communicate the company's mission, objectives, and goals to everyone within the company.

2. Make sure people at all levels within the company are talking to each other and promote the cross-pollination of ideas.

3. Create an environment that is tolerant of risk and failure.

4. Help people establish definite objectives for each development project and make sure everyone knows what they are.

5. Minimize competitive turf issues and interfunctional squabbles.

6. Make sure creative people are not bogged down with administrative office routine.

7. Recognize that creative people are different from most other people and tolerate their idiosyncrasies.

8. Provide creative people freedom to look outside the organization for important insights and stimulus.

9. Reward and recognize the creative performers in ways that are meaningful to them and don't hesitate to publicize their outstanding performance. If they are part of a team, reward the entire team.

10. Allow time and provide facilities to experiment with new ideas.

11. Encourage an informal work environment to the extent possible, allowing people to dress casually and use flexible work hours.

12. Provide fast evaluation and feedback of ideas when they are submitted.

13. Encourage people to have more than one task at a time.

14. Be willing to consider partially thought-out ideas and give people time to develop them further.

15. Encourage guided brainstorming as a means of stimulating many creative ideas in a short period of time.

16. Maintain an openness to creative ideas from outsiders, recognizing that not everything has to be invented internally.

17. Identify the winners within the company and do everything possible to motivate and keep them.

MANAGERS WHO ENCOURAGE CREATIVITY

The best managers are those who don't feel intimidated by creative people. They spur creative people on to greater performance levels than they ever thought possible. Good managers are willing to take calculated risks, and they encourage their subordinates to do the same.

Good managers recognize that there will be failures from time to time. They know that their job is to help their people get going again after they stumble. They place a high premium on learning from mistakes, and they never punish the bearer of bad news.

Managers who encourage creativity don't take very long to decide to support an idea worth pursuing. They don't require big studies before making up their minds, and they are willing to stand by their decision without waffling.

Good managers are good listeners, and they listen carefully to whatever people have to say. They recognize their own frailties, inadequacies, and vulnerabilities, and they lean upon their subordinates to help them.

KILLING CREATIVITY AND INNOVATION

In some ways, it seems much easier to kill creativity and innovation than it does to promote it. Here's how to do it.

- Set deadlines unilaterally and make them unrealistic.
- Take a long time to make go/no-go decisions.
- Analyze everything to death.
- Don't bother with a long-range strategic plan.
- Drop the ball and don't follow up.
- Don't allow travel or attendance at trade shows.
- Don't allow talking to outsiders.
- Don't give people resources to try new ideas.
- Have a lot of meetings.
- Create red tape.
- Discourage new ideas.
- Concentrate on short-term profits.
- Be very serious and formal.
- Don't have a sense of urgency about tomorrow.
- Promote functional turf wars and competitiveness.
- Don't allow risk taking and punish failure.
- Make sure everyone protects themselves with memos.
- Don't allow time to read or think.
- Punish nonconformity.
- Don't bother with recognition.

Some statements that are likely to block creativity and innovation are:

"It's ahead of the times."

"Let's put together a committee to study this."

"Our company policy won't allow this."

"I'm too busy to be bothered now."

"It's a good idea, but it's not the right time."

"We don't need something new now."

"You should be more practical."

"There's no rush."

"Let's sleep on it."

"If it's such a good idea, why hasn't someone else done it before?"

"We tried it last year and it didn't work."

"That's a really stupid idea."

"The CEO won't like it."

"You really know better."

"We don't have the time or resources."

"We're not ready for that kind of thinking."

"I'm sure it won't work."

"We're too small for this to work."

"I just know it can't work."

"You're too impractical."

"Your idea costs too much."

"I'm too busy to listen to you."

"Stop stepping on toes."

"Let's think it over for a while."

"We've never done it that way before."

These killer phrases are insidious, and they are present at all levels within the company. It takes a conscious effort to identify and eliminate them.

CREATIVITY AND INNOVATION IN LARGE COMPANIES

It seems as if it's much easier to be creative and innovative in a start-up or small company than it is in a large company. In a small company there is less red tape, the founding entrepreneur is inclined to move quickly, there is better communication between all levels, there are fewer interfering turf issues, and there is better contact with the marketplace.

Large companies have to go out of their way to promote an

entrepreneurial spirit. If they don't, all the bureaucratic controls and heavy-handed infrastructure surely will get in the way.

Raytheon Company, a very large organization, went out of its way to further the cause of creativity and innovation by setting up a New Products Center in 1969.[3] Since its inception, the center has developed more than 37 successful new products. Raytheon's investment in new product development has yielded better than a 10-to-1 return on its investment.

Raytheon's New Products Center's goal is to develop profitable new profits that further the company's growth. This is done by making sure there is the right mix of different kinds of people in an environment that encourages long-term thinking. They make sure that technical people have a good working relationship with their clients and with the marketplace. They keep all avenues of communication wide open. The New Products Center is well supported by senior management no matter what is going on in the rest of the company or the economy.

3M is another company that continues to succeed at promoting creativity and innovation. 3M expects that 30 to 35% of its sales revenues will come from products that were introduced in the prior five years. The company makes it possible to achieve this by being willing to provide adequate funding for R&D, $784 million in 1990, or 6.5% of sales. Communication between the scientists, engineers and the marketing people is encouraged. Anyone is allowed to spend up to 15% of his or her time to pursue personal research projects that are unrelated to anything else going on in the company.

General Electric has found its own way of excelling at being creative and of moving bright ideas into successful products that meet marketplace needs. GE has an R&D center in Schenectady, New York, with 1,800 researchers, 500 of whom have Ph.D.s. There, researchers are encouraged to mix with people who have different skills and interests, thus assuring the cross-pollination that is so important to creativity and innovation. They are urged to sit at different tables each week in the cafeteria to meet different people, and a number of people are transferred each year to one of the operating divisions. To help stimulate the flow of creative juices, they are treated to art exhibits and classical music concerts, and they have a regular Friday evening "free beer and pretzel party" where people can share ideas.

ALLOWING TIME TO EXPERIMENT

It's important for creative people to be allowed time to experiment and to try out their ideas, even though the ideas may seem half-baked at the time. Besides 3M, a number of companies allow people to use up to 15% of their time to pursue projects that may seem to others to be a little far- fetched.

It was 3M's 15% free-time rule that enabled Art Fry, a 3M chemical engineer, to develop the Post-it™ note pads. As noted earlier, Fry was bothered by how hard it was to mark his place in a church hymnal. The pieces of paper he used as markers always fell out when he got up to sing.

Fry found out that someone else at 3M had developed an adhesive with very poor sticking power. He thought that the adhesive could be used to make paper markers that would stick to something but later could be removed easily. Fry used his 15% free-time allowance and a grant from the company to make some prototype notepads with the adhesive. He distributed them to secretaries all over the company. They loved the notepads, and 3M later formed a very successful new business around Fry's idea.

It's not necessary for a company to have an official 15% policy, so long as it recognizes that it is appropriate for people to have time to think and not to penalize them when they appear to be looking out the window or reading a trade or technical journal.

INNOVATION GRANT PROGRAMS

An innovation grant program provides development funds that cannot be readily obtained by any other means to anyone who has an idea that seems worth pursuing. It's another way of promoting creativity and innovation because it provides a way of risk-free funding of unpopular innovation.

With an innovation grant, anyone can apply for funds by submitting a simple one- or two-page application and can secure a fast approval. The funds, anywhere from $1,000 to $200,000, can be spent in any way necessary, including market research. Typically, funds are not granted for ideas that would develop line extensions of currently existing products.

A number of companies have innovation grant programs. W. H.

Brady has its "Innovation Grant Program," 3M has its "Genesis" grants, and Teleflex has a "New Venture Fund." These programs are all designed to further creativity and innovation. Innovation grant programs are relatively informal, and the reporting requirements are minimal.

REWARDING AND MOTIVATING CREATIVITY AND INNOVATION

It used to be assumed that creative people don't need rewards, that the act of creating was sufficient reward in itself. This isn't necessarily so because, particularly with scientific and engineering work, the payoff may be far off in the future. That's why it is so important to find ways of rewarding and motivating creative people soon after their moment of inspiration. It's the best way to keep their level of interest and enthusiasm as high as possible.

Recognition Is Best

Provided people are making enough money in the first place, the consistently most motivating reward is to provide public recognition for the creative person. If someone makes an effort to submit an idea, the worst thing that can happen is for the idea to be ignored.

Hughes Aircraft Company discovered that the flow of ideas and suggestions from its engineers and scientists increased dramatically when it offered the creative people plenty of public recognition. Hughes estimates that 10 to 25% of its nearly 10,000 engineers participate in a suggestion program that rewards people with recognition.

A letter from a senior manager can be a very powerful motivator, especially if a copy of the letter is included in the creative person's personnel file. A letter in the personnel file provides a permanent record of the person's achievement, and there is a direct possibility that it will be considered favorably when it is time for salary review and promotion.

Phillips Petroleum Company has gone as far as building an advertising campaign around its most creative employees. A widely publicized ad shows pictures of particularly creative people. The ad states that the company's future depends on such employees. This is powerful motivation indeed. In addition to the promotional hype, Phillips has been providing recognition for its creative employees for many years: an estimated 400 to 500 researchers are given some sort of recognition every year for their ideas.

Reward the Team

It's always best to find ways of rewarding the entire team if it has been particularly creative in developing a project, especially if the support people are included. Singling out an individual within the team for special attention serves only to demoralize the rest of the team members and the team's effectiveness will be hampered.

Endnotes

[1] M. K. Badawy, "How to Prevent Creativity Mismanagement," *Research-Technology Management,* July 1986, pp. 45-52.

[2] D. H. Gobeli and D. J. Brown, "Analyzing Product Innovations," *Research-Technology Management,* July/August 1987, pp. 60-66.

[3] Freedman, G. "R&D in a Diverse Company: Raytheon's New Products Center," *Management Review,* Special Report, 1989, pp. 28-33.

19 The Japanese Approach to New Product Development

We hear so much about the Japanese and their unending virtues regarding product development and marketing. For the most part, we would rather not have to pay any more attention to them. But the fact is that they have had outstanding success in establishing commercially viable beachheads in a number of product areas. Thus, it pays to examine in some detail just how Japanese industry has done so well over such a relatively short period of time to see what lessons might be applicable to us.

ALLOCATION OF RESOURCES

Japan leads in its willingness and ability to allocate resources to improve its competitive position. In 1989, Japanese companies allocated $759 billion to increase their productivity and to develop new products. This was about 24% of their gross national product (GNP) for that year. During that same year, U.S. companies spent $500 billion to increase productivity and to develop new products, about 10% of U.S. GNP.[1]

The Japanese allocate their resources differently than do their counterpart companies in the United States. In the United States, two-thirds of industrial R&D expenditures go for invention, one-third to develop processes that make these products. In Japan, the reverse is true; one-third of the R&D funds go for invention, two-thirds for developing manufacturing capability. The Japanese not only do a good job of developing new products, but they also excel at manufacturing them and delivering them to their customers.

LONG-TERM VIEW

Japan's companies are patient. They take a much longer view of development time, profits, and growth than do their counterpart companies in the United States. Japan's efforts to become a major player in the aircraft industry are an example of this attitude.

The United States now has a leading position in the design and manufacturing of aircraft, but the Japanese are working hard to undermine it. Japan has worked for 30 years to build an aerospace industry, undaunted by its failures and by the intense competition of overseas manufacturers. In the late 1960s, Mitsubishi Heavy, in a consortium with other Japanese companies, built a 60-seat commercial aircraft, the YS11, but it was able to sell only 100 of them. This was a commercial failure.

The consortium didn't stop developing aircraft, though. They analyzed their problems and started again. In the United States, companies might simply have given up and gotten out of the business. Japanese industry, with support from the Japanese government, agreed to continue to develop a commercially successful aircraft.

Today, Mitsubishi Heavy and other Japanese companies manufacture major components of Boeing airplanes, and they make fighter airplanes under American licenses.

The Japanese have also been contracting to provide some of the highly advanced materials that go into modern aircraft. Their government is sponsoring research on a new kind of aircraft engine that could drive airplanes at twice the speed. The Japanese intend to become major suppliers of space satellites within the next ten years. This is truly a long-term view.

LEARNING FROM FAILURES

The Japanese don't seem to worry a whole lot if a major effort is a failure, provided they learn something in the process. Japan's fifth-generation computer project was intended to develop computers that could translate languages and understand speech. The project failed, after the expenditure of $250 million. Yet, while others might have been defeated, the Japanese learned from their mistakes. They are moving on to an even more ambitious project, an industrial effort to develop a computer architecture known as parallel processing. They are using the trained scientists and engineers and the knowledge base they gained during the fifth-generation computer project to go on to bigger and better things.

REFINED IMPROVEMENTS

The Japanese excel at converting someone else's ideas and technologies into marketable new products. They often take basic ideas that have been overlooked by others and convert them into something else. The videocassette recorder (VCR) is an example.

An American company (Ampex) developed the VCR as a product for professional use. In the early 1970s, Ampex decided not to pursue the commercialization of the VCR, leaving the field open to the Japanese. After studying consumer needs, Sony and Matsushita added a clock timer to the VCR and turned it into a consumer product. They marketed it as a device that could be used to record television programs for delayed viewing.

Consumers love their VCRs because they are free to watch their favorite TV programs whenever they want. They are no longer obligated to watch them only at show time. Today, it is virtually impossible to buy an American-made VCR. There are over 70 million VCRs in American homes and most of these are Japanese.

In fact, there is little doubt that the Japanese will continue to dominate the VCR market because they have not stopped refining current models. For instance, Matsushita Electric Industries has just developed a voice-programmable VCR. For those of us who have a terrible time trying to program our VCRs, the new VCR has a microphone and speaker built into the remote-control unit that asks for recording information orally.

The Japanese believe that it makes more sense to understand and control markets. If they do, they believe they will be more likely to have the money and the time necessary to develop new and related technologies. They believe that technology is a result of market domination, not the other way around, that without the market, there is no need for technology.

Contrary to popular American belief, the Japanese don't just copy and imitate our products. Instead, they use a sophisticated and disciplined method for converting an idea into something of commercial value. This is how they have been able to introduce totally new marketing concepts and applications to dominate a world market. They have been able to do this with tape recorders, cameras, radios, fax machines, television sets, digital watches, solar-powered calculators, a large share of the personal computer market, computer work stations, and laptop computers.

They have succeeded with more mundane, less glamorous products as well. For example, major U.S. producers of household air conditioners—Lennox, Trane, and Carrier—failed to take advantage of the ductless split, a new technology that had been invented in the United States.[2] As a result, these companies have lost an enormous market opportunity in the Far East and elsewhere as well.

The ductless split, a type of central air conditioning invented in the early 1960s, puts the compressor outside and pumps refrigerant indoors, where a fan recirculates and cools the inside air. The system pumps the refrigerant to additional fans instead of pushing chilled air through ductwork, a vastly more efficient method of cooling a whole house.

The U.S. manufacturers were not willing to invest the additional money and effort that it would take to commercialize the technology. As a result, they lost an entire market opportunity. While U.S. manufacturers now sell 37% of their air conditioner sales worldwide, Japan now sells 38%, mostly in the form of ductless splits. Carrier has less than 1% of the market in Japan. Possibly, Japan will become dominant in air conditioner sales worldwide before too long.

EXPLORATORY DEVELOPMENT

In Japan, companies are not reluctant to conduct R&D that ranges far beyond what might be expected to fit within the scope of the company.[3]

For example, Kobe Steel, Ltd., conducted a development project in wood resources that led to identifying fungi that selectively degrade 50% more wood liquor than any other microorganisms. This made it possible to produce commercial quantities of sugar and alcohol from wood.

Yokohama Rubber Company had been a major tire manufacturer for many years. It increased its R&D budget and decided to go after markets that were not directly related to tires. Now, Yokohama Rubber is selling such diverse products as electroconductive rubber for sensors, switches, membrane keyboards, and touch control applications. They also have developed a flexible printed circuit board, a microwave absorber, rubber fences, graded compression golf balls, and golf club heads.

FAST PRODUCT DEVELOPMENT

The Japanese have learned also that, even though worker's wages may be relatively high, it is possible to produce low-cost, quality goods and get them into the marketplace quickly by using a fast multifunctional parallel team approach to new product development. In a parallel team approach, all the key players of the team start with the project at the same time at the beginning of the project. Team members not only include representatives from all the contributory functional areas, but often key suppliers and customers as well. (See Chapter 3 for details on parallel product development techniques.)

In Japan, it is not uncommon for researchers to interact with product designers, engineers, marketing people, and management. The researchers visit the manufacturing facilities and design, engineering, and marketing people visit the laboratories. They are able to form teams consisting of people who really know each other, people who have shared experiences at work and at play.

Japanese companies prefer to develop and introduce products in a series of small, incremental improvements, unlike their Western counterparts who prefer to go for home runs. They have learned that small improvements in products and procedures are crucial for the ultimate success of their companies.

The Japanese have learned that the way to minimize risk with new technology is by applying the technology to fairly simple products first, to establish a position in the marketplace where minor defects are not very serious. This buys them time while they develop more sophisticated products. They typically introduce these fairly simple products into high-volume, competitive markets.

The Japanese have realized that while new technology is important, it is nowhere as important as getting products to the market first. They know that the way to grab greater market share is to get new products to the market before anyone else and to keep on delivering follow-on, improved products that have more and more features.

They also tend to rely to a far greater degree than do U.S. companies on introducing high-volume consumer products that have short life cycles. They work hard to develop sophisticated design and production techniques to make these products.

CONSTANT EVALUATION OF PROJECTS

Japanese companies make an active effort to weed out projects that have little chance of being successful, whereas American companies are more likely to take a passive approach. The Japanese frequently assess the status of their projects, relating such assessments to evaluations of the marketplace. They ask whether the market and earnings potentials justify continued outlays for the project.[4]

Development projects in many Japanese companies are evaluated regularly. The very best projects are given extra resources to push them into the marketplace sooner. The worst projects are often abandoned, and no further resources are wasted on them. Average projects are examined to see if there is a way of making them the better.

TIES TO INTERNATIONAL TRADING COMPANIES

Large Japanese manufacturing companies often are closely linked to international trading companies who provide significant marketing know-how and capabilities. The trading companies also provide a solid base of market research data, which helps the Japanese manufacturing companies understand international marketplace needs.

AVAILABILITY OF MAJOR FUNDING

Japanese industrial companies have much more money to invest in their own projects and capital development than have their U.S. counterparts. Most of the Japanese companies have strong ties to Japanese banks and other financial institutions who have always been ready to provide funds to their clients. This is a significant advantage for Japanese companies because it means that whenever they have identified a market opportunity and have developed a product to meet that need, they know that they will have plenty of money to move forward aggressively.

Investment money also is available for foreign investment. For example, a number of U.S. biotechnology companies have discovered that, while they have found it very hard to get additional financing from domestic sources, there has been plenty of money available from Japan.

GOVERNMENT POLICIES THAT FAVOR PRODUCT DEVELOPMENT AND TRADE

A major difference between Japan and the United States relates to the Japanese government's willingness, and the U.S. government's unwillingness, to develop a national industrial policy that creates and protects new industries and their technologies until they are positioned competitively in the marketplace.

The Japanese government gets deeply involved in setting policy for the growth of its industry, primarily through the actions of its Ministry of International Trade and Industry (MITI). In contrast, with regard to U.S. industry, the U.S. government takes a hands-off policy and seems unwilling to help U.S. industry directly, although, indirectly, the U.S. government, through the Defense Department's Defense Advanced Research Projects Agency (DARPA), has helped finance a number of basic technologies that have proven to be of significant value to U.S. industry.

Japan's government favors a strategy that promotes innovation and applied research. MITI has supported such projects as a superhigh-performance computer for scientific applications (at a cost of nearly $30 million) and a project to develop computer technology for the recognition and processing of speech, characters, and objects (at a cost of over $100 million). It has also sponsored other projects; an electric car, low pollution steel manufacturing, laser welding technologies, and flexible manufacturing.

The help provided by DARPA is largely devoted to developing basic technologies. It does not support the development of new products that can be commercialized readily into major, competitive industries. Japan's MITI devotes itself to underwriting the cost of developing whole new industries that can compete in world markets.

Another important point is that, after World War II, the Japanese government urged manufacturing companies to concentrate their efforts on developing products for export. Over the ensuing years, this has made it much easier for Japanese companies to penetrate the U.S. market with products that are designed for the needs of the export market. The United States, on the other hand, tries to sell products designed for the domestic trade into international markets, with less than stunning success.

Further, the Japanese government fosters the development of national technologies, and it supports conglomerate structures, *keiretsu*, that can sustain significant losses while developing new technologies into marketable products.

The Japanese government supported Nippon Telegraph and Telephone Corporation (NTT) during its early days in the 1950s. It provided a national policy that was favorable to the development of telecommunications and an environment that was hostile to competition. As a result, by the late 1980s, NTT became Japan's largest company and the world's second largest telecommunications company, with consolidated revenues of $38 billion and total assets of $70 billion.

The Japanese have learned that an all-out, multicompany, government sponsored development of a technology will lead to major breakthroughs and related technologies that can be converted into marketable products.

JAPAN'S PATENT LAWS

Japan's patent laws also are very favorable to Japanese industry and unfavorable to companies from other countries. In Japan, the information contained in a patent application filed by a company in another country is published immediately after the application is filed. If the idea seems to be a good one, the Japanese government will often delay the patent approval. At the same time, it helps Japanese industry to develop similar technologies and products.

Allied-Signal, an American company, spent 15 years and over $100 million to develop a new metal alloy made of iron, silicon, and boron that had properties of both glass and metal.[5] The new metal, "Metglas," cuts energy losses in electrical transformers by 70%. It has been unable to sell the alloy to Japanese utilities because the Japanese government blocked the issuance of Allied-Signal's patent for 12 years. During this time, Japanese companies were given a government subsidy to develop a similar product.

Motorola faced a similar situation when it was blocked from marketing its palm-size Micro-TAC cellular telephone in Japan. While the Japanese patent office held up Motorola's patent application, Matsushita Electric Industries came out with an even smaller version of the same product.

BASIC RESEARCH

Basic research is essential for the future because it ultimately drives economic growth. It is important that the United States continue to conduct the basic research that will lead to new technologies. But the United States does not appear to be as interested in converting basic technology into marketable new products as the Japanese who, time and time again, do a better job of converting someone else's basic research into valuable products.

In the United States, most of the basic research is done at the universities. Student and faculty publications are available to anyone who wants to read them. U.S. industry conducts very little basic research because of its high costs and uncertain outcome. This is reversed in Japan where most of the basic research is conducted by industry. The results are not shared with anyone else unless MITI decides that it is in the best interest of the country that the technology be shared with other companies.

The Defense Department's Advanced Research Agency (DARPA) has financed a number of basic technologies. Among these are computerized machine tools, integrated circuits, advanced composite materials, supercomputers, specialized optics, and telecommunications. Unfortunately, developing the basic technologies is not enough. Converting them into marketable and commercially successful products is essential, and this is where Japan excels.

CULTURAL DIFFERENCES

The Japanese and other Asian manufacturing companies can also count on the fact that there are significant cultural differences between the people in their countries and those of the Western countries. Asian people are more inclined to work well in teams, taking a view that the group well-being is more important than that of the individual. Americans, in particular, are more inclined to see things differently, namely, that the individual is more important than the group. It appears that Americans are still wanting to be rugged individualists, as if they were still settling the Wild West.

The implications are important. If American manufacturing companies want to stress the importance of multifunctional teams and compete with the Japanese, they will have to find ways of dealing with the fact that their prospective team members don't necessarily have a natural inclination to work well together.

Endnotes

[1] "Japan Keeps Up the Big Spending to Maintain Its Industrial Might," *The New York Times,* April 11, 1990, p. A1.

[2] "How Japan is Beating the Others Cold," *Business Week,* September 3, 1990, p. 79.

[3] Herbert, E. "How Japanese Companies Set R&D Directions," *Research-Technology Management,* September-October, 1990, pp. 28-37.

[4] Balachandra, R. "Winning the Race to the Marketplace," *The Wall Street Journal,* April 30, 1990, p. A14.

[5] Magnusson, P. and Gross, N. "Japan's Latest End-Run Around Free Trade," *Business Week,* October 1, 1990, p. 32.

20 Research and Development Management

Every member of a multifunctional new product development team contributes something special to the process. Each has unique talents and skills and all are necessary and important in their own way. Research and Development is particularly important because it represents the greatest repository of technological knowledge and skills within the company. R&D's ability to contribute to the new product development process is dependent upon how well it manages its own activities and how much time it has to devote to new product development projects.

R&D'S ROLE WITHIN THE COMPANY

The R&D department of a company has to be responsive to senior management, external customers, new product development teams, and other internal customers such as Manufacturing, Quality Assurance, Engineering, Marketing, and Sales. R&D has a number of specific tasks:

- Tracking emerging technology
- Providing technical problem solving
- Developing new products and processes

- Identifying of alternate raw materials
- Performing new product feasibility studies
- Participating in new product development teams

How well R&D manages to juggle all of its responsibilities will determine how well it is able to meet the needs of the company.

R&D AND NEW PRODUCT DEVELOPMENT

While all R&D activities are important to the company, none are more important in the long run than those that relate to new product development. Yet it often happens that new product development receives inadequate attention.

The typical R&D department operates under a constant state of siege. Its people are under intense pressure to put out fires which, if not extinguished promptly, would cause serious difficulties for the company. Customer problems, manufacturing problems, product and incoming material defects, and process development all demand full attention from R&D. As a result, despite their good intentions, R&D people often have very little time left to devote to new product development projects.

An R&D department will have time only for product development if it manages all its work as effectively as possible.

SUGGESTIONS FOR IMPROVEMENT

The following are some suggestions for improving R&D project management effectiveness:

Strategic Planning

Many R&D departments seem to operate by crisis management; that is, problems are tackled as they come in, with those making the loudest noise getting the greatest attention. This leaves R&D in a strictly reactive mode, one that makes certain that R&D never has time for long-term new product development projects.

The way to solve this problem is for R&D to have its own strategic plan, a plan that clearly sets forth all of R&D's responsibilities and tasks. In addition to detailing R&D's objectives, goals, and strategies, its strategic plan should state what percentage of its time will be devoted to each of its activities. For example,

R&D Activity	Time Allocation
New product development	40%
Technical/manufacturing support	30%
Customer support	15%
Miscellaneous	15%

R&D should negotiate its proposed time allocation formula with senior management and with each of the functional areas. R&D should insist that new product development is important to the long-term survival and growth of the company.

Once there is agreement on the way R&D ought to spend its time, R&D will have a strategic plan that helps it focus on its long-term objectives. R&D will be less likely to operate in an environment of crisis management and knee-jerk reactivity and will be able to devote more of its efforts to new product development.

Concentrating on Projects That Have a Commercial Objective

Sometimes, R&D departments tackle projects that are not based on satisfying either a marketplace or a manufacturing need. This dilutes R&D's effectiveness because these projects have little long-term value to the company.

It's important that R&D work on small, medium, and large projects that have a commercial objective, projects that are driven by the needs of their marketplace. R&D should review its work load from time to time and make a conscious effort to weed out those projects that are on the list just because they are interesting or projects for which the marketplace need has long since disappeared.

Critical Path Project Management

Using critical path analysis to identify milestones and manage projects will go a long way to improve the effectiveness of R&D's activities. Many R&D people resist the idea of critical path management because they think it will block their creativity. The reverse is true; people who understand and manage project milestones are more likely to be creative because they will be less tense about their work.

Selecting R&D Projects

R&D tends to take on projects as the need occurs, most often in response to a problem somewhere in the company. There is little effort to take a proactive role in determining what R&D ought to be doing to serve the long-term best interests on the company. Because it is usually somewhat isolated from the Manufacturing and Marketing activities of the company, R&D often is the last to know what will serve the company best.

Since manufacturing and marketing people are directly affected by R&D's activities, it helps if they have a say in what R&D does. A team, comprised of a qualified person each from Manufacturing, Marketing, and R&D, should help select the type of projects R&D takes on. Each team member should have a broad view of the company's business and its marketplace niche and should recognize R&D's important role in the company.

Project categories that are selected by the multifunctional team will help assure that R&D's projects are relevant. R&D will have less of its time taken up by meaningless projects and will have more time to devote to new product development activities.

Improving Communication and Technology Transfer

Many R&D projects fail or turn out to be irrelevant because R&D people do not communicate adequately with people in the rest of the company. Project management will be more effective if the R&D staff consistently and effectively communicates with manufacturing, marketing, quality assurance, and another technical people within the company. R&D people will have a better idea of the needs of the company and will be able to receive helpful suggestions on how to speed up a project or how to make it more meaningful.

Good communication also is the basis of good technology transfer. Without suppliers and users of new technology talking to each other on a regular basis, there can be no effective technology transfer.

Potential users of the new technology have to be willing to

receive it and to begin applying it within their areas. When a new technology has been developed by R&D, it is a good idea to transfer an R&D person along with the new technology to the area within the company where the new process is being applied.

Knowing When to Quit

Technical people have a tendency to continue a project far too long, even if it is no longer technologically feasible. They believe in the deepest recesses of their minds that technical success is just around the corner, that success will be possible if only they keep plugging away for just a few more months. While this is sometimes true, there is a point of diminishing return past which it no longer pays to continue a project that will only waste people's time and cause intense anguish.

Management of Technology Information

The management of technology information is extremely important.

It's easy to find information about new technological advances because they appear in print everywhere. The problem is that there is so much of it. The amount of information on technological change is staggering, and it is growing at a faster rate than anyone can even begin to imagine.

For the information to do any good within the company, it must be funnelled to the right people. New product development teams, in particular, need a constant flow of useful information about technological developments if they are to succeed with their projects.

Allied Corporation has attempted to deal with the flow of technology information by appointing a scientist with broad interests to be a "technology gate keeper." The gate keeper's charter is to assist other scientists in solving difficult technical problems and to monitor incoming technology. While this has worked for Allied, there are not too many companies that have such a senior scientist who can fill this role.

Alternatively, another approach would be to appoint a special team (a "technology triage team") whose role would be to monitor any technologies that might be of value to the company. In particular, they would feed potentially useful information to product development teams. This team would be comprised of a person each from R&D, Manufacturing, and Engineering. The team's members would serve a two-year assignment on the team, and new people could be assigned to the team on a rotating basis.

Travel to Customer Locations

R&D people commonly are isolated from the mainstream, rarely having an opportunity to learn about marketplace needs or field use conditions firsthand. When this is the case, their projects may have little relationship to the needs of the marketplace.

It's a good practice to send R&D people into the field as often as possible so that they can learn about customers' needs directly. Outside travel makes it more likely that their projects will have real meaning. Their people will be more creative because their thinking will have been stimulated by different experiences.

THE ROLE OF CORPORATE R&D

Many otherwise decentralized companies benefit by having a corporate R&D department. Because it has a pool of technical talent and is in a central location, a corporate R&D department can help the divisions and serve the company in a number of ways by

- Facilitating technology transfer
- Guiding the new product development process
- Developing new products and processes
- Providing training
- Identifying and championing new technologies
- Advising senior management on technical matters
- Providing an incubator for special projects
- Providing technical assistance when needed
- Monitoring technologies to identify those that are becoming obsolete
- Supplying ideas

Corporate R&D can offer significant help to the divisions, but, unfortunately, the help is not often accepted. The divisions often view corporate R&D as an unnecessary cash drain that they are obligated to support. Because corporate R&D tends to conduct long-term projects that have little chance of immediate payoff, the divisions are unable to understand corporate R&D's importance to the company. This is an age-old problem for which there are no easy solutions.

Corporate R&D must continually seek to educate the divisions on its value and to provide the divisions with services at every opportunity. It must continue to demonstrate that it is capable of making decisions that are based on sound business principles.

21 Product Development in the Decentralized Company

A decision is usually made to decentralize a company when it is apparent that it can be divided into business units that differ from each other on a logical basis. This is usually done when the business units have well-differentiated markets and product lines. When the decision to decentralize has been made, it is usually assumed that each of the divisions will be responsible for its own new product development. It is argued that separated divisions can move fast, will take greater ownership of the new product idea, and will have better control over the project.

PRODUCT DEVELOPMENT PROBLEMS THAT AFFLICT A DECENTRALIZED COMPANY

The benefits notwithstanding, a decentralized company can have problems that interfere with new product development. Some of these problems are the following:

Competition for Resources

In a decentralized company, the divisions compete with each other for scarce resources, such as money, facilities, equipment, and manpower.

The divisions also compete for senior management's attention. Division management usually has little opportunity to visit with the company's senior management. Senior management may have difficulty being able to transmit its sense of commitment and urgency about new product development to the divisions. Conversely, division managers may be unable to approach corporate senior management with their ideas.

Short-Range Tactical Thinking

The divisions are under intense pressure to achieve their targets for profits. As a result of this orientation, they tend to take a short-term view that is dictated by their quarterly profit performance. They are apt to concentrate on the relatively easy development projects, routine matters, and service activities that have a greater likelihood of immediate payoff. They tend to ignore those longer-range and more difficult projects that could be of great importance to the division in the long run.

Division general managers are prone to believing that day to day putting out fires is more important than new product development. They are reluctant to commit scarce resources to something that doesn't have the potential for immediate payout. This is an attitude problem that can lead to a direct conflict with the people in the division who are entrusted with new product development. R&D and other people who push for new product development sometimes are viewed in negative terms as nonteam players. Bitterness and frustration abound under such circumstances and little of any real value is accomplished.

Small Pool of Ideas

A small division is not likely to produce a large number of ideas or have direct access to ideas from other divisions or from elsewhere in the company. Because it has few ideas, the small division is apt to concentrate on line extensions or modifications of currently existing products as opposed to developing truly new products that might have a substantial positive impact on the division's future.

Inadequate Market Research

In a small division, the distinction between Marketing and Sales often becomes blurred or nonexistent. Marketing people sometimes have to spend a lot of time putting out fires which, in a larger division or in a centralized company, would ordinarily be handled by sales people or sales representatives. This becomes problematic when the marketing people have little time or inclination to conduct the market research that is so essential for good new product development. In such circumstances, the division becomes sales or customer driven (reactive), as opposed to being market driven (proactive) and new product development suffers.

Poor Technology Transfer

It's unusual for good technology transfer to occur between the divisions in a decentralized company. This is because of such issues as

- The "not invented here" syndrome
- Poor communication between the divisions
- A lack of awareness that the technology developed at one division might be useful elsewhere within the company

It often happens that a division wastes time trying to solve a problem when the solution is readily available at another division.

Emphasis on Process Development

R&D departments within divisions spend much of their time solving production problems. After a while, they see this as their primary reason for existence. Under these circumstances, unless they make a special effort to the contrary, they become process oriented and are unable to devote resources or time to new product development. A certain amount of process development is important, provided an appropriate amount of effort is devoted to new product development.

Inadequate Resources

A small division will have a hard time finding adequate resources for its new product development teams. Often, such equipment as personal computers, test equipment, CAD equipment, and good software are unavailable to a division because it has to spend its money in other ways. Fast new product development suffers because development teams cannot do well without plenty of resources.

Poor Accounting Feedback

In a decentralized company, accounting departments are often at the corporate offices. The divisions typically have a controller or accountant who is overburdened with record keeping and who has little time or inclination to keep track of the costs incurred by specific development projects.

Development teams need to have up-to-date information on how well they are controlling their costs. If such information is not readily available to them, they can incur a cost overrun without being aware of it. To get around this problem, the development team often has to do its own accounting and this is a wasteful use of the team's time.

Isolation

Divisions are often located in small communities far away from the company's corporate headquarters, and they are distant from the other divisions. They tend to be very isolated, and they suffer all the effects of isolation. It's difficult for them to learn of or understand important changes in company direction, and they are often the last to hear about significant policy decisions.

Part of the problem is that, after prolonged isolation, the divisions no longer know the key corporate players within the company. They are not any longer in the power-dealing and decision-making loop. It becomes harder for them to get approval to embark on an important development project or to get a go-ahead for a major expenditure associated with a new product introduction.

Being Too Close to the Corporate Office

Being too close to the corporate offices can be worse than being too far away. Sometimes, a division is located in very close proximity to the corporate office, in the same town or even in the same building.

This poses a problem for the unfortunate division because there is no way it can escape from the constant watch and second-guessing of its corporate parents. In such instances, senior management is apt to get too involved and not let the divisions conduct their own affairs.

Unwillingness to Ask for Help

Divisions are inclined to have a feeling of independence and pride. They believe that they can do it all themselves. They are less likely to seek help when they need it because they believe they have to be on their own and because their pride prevents them from reaching out.

Because of this fiercely independent attitude, they are forced to rely on talents and skills that sometimes are less than enough for the task at hand, especially a complicated development project. Further, people in the divisions sometimes are not even aware that they need help or that help could be available from elsewhere in the company.

Too Many Rules

The corporate headquarters of decentralized companies often imposes too much bureaucracy on the divisions. This is an attempt to maintain a sense of order. Enormous bureaucracies can develop, and the division spends a major portion of its time following silly rules, filling out mountains of forms, and adhering to procedures that are totally meaningless. Excessive red tape makes it hard for the divisions to do effective new product development because the development teams have to devote so much time to satisfying the rules.

Punishing the Division That Is Doing Well

A division that is meeting all its targets for revenues and profits often has to help carry the divisions that are doing poorly. Money that would otherwise be available for new product development at the division that is performing well is drained away to help the poor performers.

ADVANTAGES OF PRODUCT DEVELOPMENT IN A DECENTRALIZED COMPANY

Despite all the possible stumbling blocks just described, there can be definite advantages to being a division within a decentralized company. Some of these are the following.

Ability to Move Faster

The division is capable of moving a lot faster than can a centralized company, especially when it comes to selecting and starting a development project that it thinks will be of real benefit. Further, once having decided to go forward with a development project, the division general manager can allocate all available resources to the project. If so inclined, the general manager can make things happen very rapidly and clear away any possible stumbling blocks for the development team.

Less Bureaucracy from Within

If it is left pretty much to its own devices, a division can operate very efficiently, with a minimum of bureaucracy. Because of its size and the close proximity of its key players, it's easier to get decisions made and a lot of unnecessary paperwork can be avoided. Go/no-go decisions are more easily made when development teams reach key project milestones.

Better Opportunity to Resolve Conflict

It's inevitable that there will be conflict in any group of people, especially if they are thrust together in small divisions. Yet, because the management of a small division is more aware of the conflict, it is easier to deal with it when it emerges.

Closer Contact with the Marketplace

The people at a division have an opportunity to be much closer to their marketplace than is often the case in a centralized company. They hear faster about product problems, and likewise, they can learn faster about opportunities for new products. Since fast product development must begin with an understanding of the needs of the marketplace, closer contact with the customers makes it more likely that those needs will be identified quickly and suitable development projects will be started.

Evaluating Your Company's New Product
22 Development Readiness

The following is a list of questions that can be used to evaluate your company's readiness to conduct effective new product development. The questions require only a yes or no answer.

NEW PRODUCT DEVELOPMENT READINESS AUDIT

1. Strategic Planning

> Does the company have a strategic plan?
>
> Is the plan widely distributed?
>
> Is there a strategic plan for new product development?
>
> Is the plan widely distributed?

2. Senior Management Involvement and Commitment

> Is senior management committed to fast new product development?
>
> Has senior management communicated a sense of urgency about new product development?

Does senior management get involved in negotiating product features and benefits, objectives, and milestones at the beginning of each major project?

Are enough funds made available for new product development?

3. Idea Generation

Do ideas for new products come from a diversity of sources?

Are there enough ideas for new products?

Are ideas acknowledged promptly?

Are they good ideas? Is there a formal program for handling ideas?

Are ideas evaluated by a team including people from Marketing, Manufacturing, Engineering, and R&D?

Are good ideas rewarded?

Is there guided brainstorming to get a lot of ideas?

Are shelved ideas reexamined annually?

4. Project Selection and Prioritization

Are there formal criteria for selecting new projects?

Are the criteria widely distributed?

Were the criteria established by a team including Marketing, Manufacturing, Engineering, R&D, and senior management?

Are the criteria updated annually?

Are there written criteria for prioritizing projects?

Are concepts for new products evaluated by a team?

Is there a way of evaluating when a project should be ended?

Has it been easy to kill a project that isn't going anywhere?

Is there a mixture of small, medium, and large projects?

5. Market Research

Is there an active program to identify marketplace needs?

Are key customers identified and visited?

Do technical, manufacturing, and marketing people visit the key customers?

Are the first few customers for a new product specifically identified?

Do technical people attend focus group meetings?

Are customer complaint data collected and analyzed?

Is there adequate market research at the beginning of each project?

6. *Specifications of New Products*

Are product features and design specifications decided by a team?

Are product features and design specifications frozen early?

Is there a program for developing incremental product improvements?

Does development aim for more "base hits" than "big hits"?

Are product features based on an actual customer needs?

7. *Project Timeliness*

Do new products reach the marketplace on schedule?

Are schedules established by the development team?

Are the milestones identified and is there a list of all the tasks?

Is computer-driven critical path management practiced?

8. *Product Development Procedures*

Do procedures for fast product development exist?

Are they well known and followed?

Are the project mission and objectives clearly defined at the beginning of the project?

Is there always an adequate preproduction piloting period after tooling has been installed?

Are project meetings milestone as opposed to calendar driven?

Is there outside sourcing of new products and designs?

Is fast parallel product development a standard practice?

Is there a project champion for each major project?

Is a simplified version of quality function deployment (QFD) used at the beginning of a project?

Are business plans prepared for major development projects?

Is there a companywide flow chart for new product development?

Are project costs closely monitored?

Does the company culture support the multifunctional team concept?

9. *Product Development Teamwork*

Are there product development teams?

Are all the key functional areas represented on the teams?

Are there team leaders?

Are the leaders chosen by the team?

Are development team members co-located?

Does each team create its own operating ground rules?

Are there rewards and incentives for teams?

Do the teams participate in project planning at the start of the project?

Are key suppliers and customers on the teams?

Do the teams have the necessary resources?

10. *Cost and Duration Estimation and Control*

Are project costs and duration estimated?

Are estimates done by a team?

Have the estimates been accurate?

Are estimates revised at key milestones?

Are cost control procedures in place?

Do team leaders know their project costs on an ongoing basis?

11. *Barriers to New Product Development*

Are there very few significant barriers to fast product development?

Does the company have a track record of fast product development?

Are there good relationships between technical, marketing, and manufacturing personnel?

Are development teams for major projects protected from interruptions?

Is there a minimum amount of bureaucracy?

Does the company take a long-term view of profits?

12. *Profit Margins*

Are profit margins for new products spelled out?

Are the expected margins reasonable?

Have new products met anticipated margin requirements?

13. *New Product Quality*

Do the new products meet high quality and reliability standards?

Are new product designs readily manufacturable?

Are there few product problems after a product has been introduced?

14. *Creativity and Innovation*

Do people know what the company's goals are?

Are risks and failures tolerated?

Is there an entrepreneurial climate?

Do people have ample time to think?

Is there an innovation grant program?

Is there a minimum of anxiety?

15. *Training Programs*

Are there training programs for fast product development?

Are there training programs for team participation and management?

16. *Technology and Design Capabilities*

Does the company have adequate technology and design capabilities?

Does the company know where to go to get outside design and development capabilities?

Does R&D have time for new product development?

Is the company geared up for fast prototyping?

Scoring:

Total number of questions = 95

Yes =

No =

Score expressed as percentage (Yes answers/95 · 100) =

A score of 75% or better indicates that the company is well on its way to achieving effective new product development. A lower score means that the company had better improve its procedures and policies.

23 Pulling It All Together

This chapter provides a summary of the important things that are worth remembering when setting up a program for fast new product development.

1. Make a big deal out the importance of accelerating the pace of new product development, making sure that everyone in the company gets the message, again and again.

2. Recognize that the switch to fast parallel product development won't be easy, that it may take years to accomplish.

3. Believe that speed is a strategic weapon than can be used to gain a competitive advantage. Speedy new product development with multifunctional teams will yield products that are first in the marketplace. These products will have higher gross margins and profits, will command higher prices and products, will be easier to manufacture, and will have fewer design flaws.

4. Understand that while speed is vital, it is not enough to get a product to the marketplace first. The product must also satisfy a real marketplace need and meet customer expectations. It must be of high quality, it must perform well, and it must meet cost requirements.

5. Develop a strategic plan for fast product development that is tied to the company's strategic plan. Emphasize strategic as opposed to tactical planning. Base strategies on core technologies and

capabilities and build more capabilities. Don't go too far afield from the company's mission and skills.

6. Use a multifunctional parallel team approach to new product development, making sure that the right people are on the team and that they all start on the project at the same time. Be sure not to disband the team until the product's manufacturing problems have been solved.

7. Concentrate on "singles" and "doubles" as opposed to "home runs," but maintain a portfolio of projects that allows for both. Remember that it is less risky to capture market share with a series of related products than it is try to go for a home run. Never stop developing new products.

8. Couple fast new product development with fast manufacturing start-up and fast product shipping. There's no point in developing products quickly if they can't be made and placed in the customer's hands very quickly.

9. Always allow for an adequate preproduction piloting period after new tooling and machinery have been installed to debug the process and to train the employees.

10. Take a long view of new product development, making sure that, to the extent possible, project funding is independent of company profits.

11. When developing a product, take advantage of processes, materials, and components that already exist within the company. Don't feel the need to reinvent the wheel every time.

12. Make sure development teams have the power to make decisions and to make things happen. See to it that the teams have all the resources they need and that there is a way of rewarding them for superior performance.

13. Don't forget to include key suppliers and, sometimes, key customers on the new product development teams.

14. Concentrate on developing products that satisfy specific marketplace needs, recognizing that products in search of a marketplace rarely go anywhere.

15. Establish a review board (new product development committee), a senior management group whose function it is to select and

prioritize new product development projects and to monitor their progress.

16. Get a fast start at parallel new product development and overcome inertia by starting and completing a small demonstration project to serve as proof that multifunctional teams are the way to go. Select a project that really means something to the company, a project that can be completed within nine months or less.

17. Make a serious effort to discover marketplace needs by conducting focus groups, by talking to the customers, by analyzing marketplace trends, by identifying problems with current products, by learning from competitors, and by systematically collecting data from customer contacts.

18. Formalize the criteria that are to be used to select development projects and make sure that everyone involved in new product development within the company is familiar with the criteria.

19. Encourage the flow of ideas for new products by acknowledging ideas promptly and rewarding good ideas when they result in products that are profitable.

20. Reward and motivate product development teams, not individuals within the teams. Remember that public recognition is a very important motivator and, provided people are adequately paid in the first place, that recognition is a better reward than money.

21. Identify the barriers to fast product development and fast manufacturing start-up and work hard to overcome them.

22. Freeze new product features and design specifications as early as possible in the development program and keep them frozen. If there is a tendency or strong desire to change the features or specifications, consider disbanding the project and starting again.

23. Use a simplified version of quality function deployment to define customer needs and to relate these needs to product features and design specifications.

24. Remember that the process by which a new product will be made is just as important as the product itself. The manufacturing

process should be developed at the same time the new product is being developed.

25. Make sure that teams are led by someone selected by the team, a person with a vision and experience in managing teams, someone who has a passionate desire for the project's success, someone with political savvy.

26. Periodically reexamine shelved ideas for new products to determine whether they are now appropriate. Often ideas that were no good yesterday are appropriate today because of changing market conditions or the appearance of a new technology.

27. Make sure technical people have a good grasp of the marketplace and of use conditions of the company's products.

28. Help forge the link between technical and marketing and sales people by encouraging them to have shared experiences; have technical people visit the marketplace with the sales staff and have sales and marketing people visit the laboratories and plants.

29. Stress marketplace pull for most of the development projects, but don't lose sight of emerging technologies that might yield new products. Remember that the management of technology is as important as the technology itself.

30. Do everything possible to break down interfunctional barriers and improve the flow of information throughout the company.

31. Use computer-driven critical path management of development projects to help identify tasks, milestones, and resources required and to provide schedules for project completion.

32. Use business plans for major projects to help crystallize ideas, to help determine if a project is worth doing, to create a plan for the project, to consider possible risks, to describe resources required, and to identify benchmarks for measuring project progress.

33. Be aware that it is appropriate to kill a development project that doesn't seem to be going anywhere, especially if the development team has lost faith in the project, if the technology is unattainable, or if the marketplace need is no longer there.

34. Encourage and nurture entrepreneurial spirit, creativity, and inno-

vation. Provide an environment that is tolerant of risk and failure and be willing to learn from mistakes.

35. Maintain a sense of humor. You'll need it because humor eases the tensions that normally accompany new product development. Humor also removes some of the constraints that ordinarily stifle creativity and innovation.

References

BOOKS

Aubrey, C.A., and P.K. Felkins. *Teamwork: Involving People in Quality and Productivity Improvement*. Milwaukee: Quality Press, ASQC, 1988.

Bossert, J.L. *Quality Function Deployment*. New York: Marcel Dekker, 1991.

Cooper, R.G. *Winning at New Products*. Reading, MA: Addison-Wesley, 1986.

Marrus, S.K. *Building the Strategic Plan*. New York: John Wiley, 1984.

Miller, W.C. *The Creative Edge*. Reading, MA: Addison-Wesley, 1987.

Rosenau, M.D. *Faster New Product Development*. New York: AMACOM, 1990.

Rubenstein, A.H. *Managing Technology in the Decentralized Firm*. New York: Wiley-Interscience, 1989.

Smith, P.G., and D.G. Reinertsen. *Developing Products in Half the Time*. New York: Van Nostrand Reinhold, 1991.

Stalk, G., Jr., and T.M. Hout. *Competing Against Time*. New York: Free Press, 1990.

Tatsuno, S.M. *Created in Japan: From Imitators to World-Class Innovators*. New York: Harper & Row, 1990.

ARTICLES

Abelson, P.H. "America Bashing," *Science*, June 8, 1990, p. 1173.

Abetti, P.A., and R.W. Stuart. "Evaluating New Product Risk," *Research-Technology Management*, May/June 1988, pp. 100–103.

Adams, R.M., and M.D. Gavoor. "Quality Function Deployment: Its Promise and Reality," *Quality Digest,* July 1990, pp. 19–36.

Adler, P.S., H.E. Riggs, and S.C. Wheelright. "Product Development Know-How: Trading Tactics for Strategy," *Sloan Management Review,* Fall 1989, pp. 7–17.

Andrews, E.L. "Translated, HDTV Means 'Beat Japan'," *Business Month,* June, 1990, pp. 67–69.

Ashley, S. "The Battle to Build Better Products," *Mechanical Engineering,* November 1990, pp. 34–38.

Badawy, M.K. "How to Prevent Creativity Mismanagement," *Research-Technology Management,* July 1986, pp. 45–52.

Baker, N.R., S.G. Green, and A.S. Bean. "How Management Can Influence the Generation of Ideas," *Research-Technology Management,* December 1985.

Balachandra, R., and J.A. Raelin. "When to Kill That R&D Project," *Research-Technology Management,* July/August 1984, pp. 9–12.

Balachandra, R. "Winning the Race to the Marketplace," *The Wall Street Journal,* April 30, 1990.

Becker, R.H., L.S. Crawley, and R.J. Little. "Have You Looked into Your Pool of Unexploited Technology Lately?" *Research-Technology Management,* May/June 1989, pp. 3–5.

Boulton, W.R. "Japanese Approach to Innovation," *les Nouvelles,* March 1990, pp. 11–14.

Bradsher, K. "Beating Japan at Its Own Game," *The New York Times,* July 13, 1990.

Brenner, M.S. "R&D Cut Before—Not After—Acquisition," *Research-Technology Management,* May/June 1990, pp. 15–18.

Buell, B. "Sculley: Up Against the Lab Wall," *Business Week,* October 15, 1990, p. 92.

Buggie, F.D. "Broaden the Search for Clues to Product Commercialization," *Journal of Business Strategy,* November/December 1989, pp. 37–40.

Burrill, G. S. "Managing the Technical Professional: A Question of Balance," *Management Review,* Special Report, 1989, pp. 24–27.

Carroll, P. B. "IBM Again Delays Its Entry into Market for Laptop PC's," *The Wall Street Journal,* October 9, 1990.

Chay, R. F. "Discovering Unrecognized Needs with Consumer Research" *Research-Technology Management,* March/April 1989, pp. 36–39.

Clark, K. B. "What Strategy Can Do for Technology" *Harvard Business Review,* November/December 1989, pp. 94–98.

Collier, D. W., J. Monz, and J. Conlin. "How Effective is Technological Innovation?" *Research-Technology Management,* October 1984.

"Computers and Other Targets: How Japan Learns and Wins, Even by Losing," *The New York Times,* May 10, 1990.

"Concurrent Engineering, Global Competitiveness, and Staying Alive: An

Industrial Management Roundtable," *Industrial Management,* July/August 1990, pp. 6–16.

Cooper, R. G. "New Products: What Distinguishes the Winners," *Research-Technology Management,* November/December 1990, pp. 27–31.

Cooper, R. G. "New Product Performance and Product Innovation Strategies," *Research-Technology Management,* May/June 1986, pp. 35–43.

Crow, M. M., and B. L. Bozeman, "Bureaucratization in the Laboratory," *Research-Technology Management,* September/October 1989, pp. 29–30.

Dertouzos, M. L. "Commission Report: Made in America," *The Commonwealth Newsletter,* April 16, 1990, pp. 226–231.

Drucker, P. F. "Marketing 101 for a Fast-Changing Decade," *The Wall Street Journal,* November 29, 1990.

Drucker, P. F. "Best R&D Is Business Driven," *The Wall Street Journal,* February 10, 1988.

Dumaine, B. "How Managers Can Succeed Through Speed," *Fortune,* January 13, 1989.

Dumaine, R. "Who Needs a Boss?" *Fortune,* May 7, 1990, pp. 52–60.

Ellis, L. W., and R. G. McDonald. "Reforming Management Accounting to Support Today's Technology," *Research-Technology Management,* March/April 1990, pp. 30–34.

Ettlie, J. E. "What Makes a Manufacturing Firm Innovative?" *Academy of Management Executives,* Vol. 4, No. 4, 1990, pp. 7–19.

Farnsworth, C. H. "Report Warns of Decline of U.S. Electronics Industry," *The New York Times,* June 9, 1990.

Fischer, W. A., W. Hamilton, C. P. McLaughlin, and R. W. Zaud. "The Elusive Product Champion," *Research-Technology Management,* May/June 1986, pp. 31–34.

"Follow-through: 3M's Formula for Success," *R&D Magazine,* November 1990, pp. 46–52.

Foran, P. "Team Approach to Manufacturing Speeds New Products to Market," *The Business Journal,* May 28, 1990, pp.. 14–15.

Foster, R. N., L. H. Linden, R. L. Whitely, and A. M. Kantrow. "Improving the Return on R&D-II," *Research-Technology Management,* March 1985.

Freedman, G. "R&D in a Diverse Company: Raytheon's New Products Center," *Management Review,* Special Report, 1989, pp. 28–33.

Frumerman, R. "Ten Commandments for Successful Development," *Research-Technology Management,* July/August 1990, pp. 10–11.

Gates, M. "Spurring Innovation," *Incentive,* October 1989, pp. 49–51.

Gaynor, G. H. "Selecting Projects," *Research-Technology Management,* July/August 1990, pp. 43–45.

Glover, R. J. "Cultivating the Innovative Process," *Chemtech,* April 1989, pp. 221–225.

Gobeli, D. H., and D. J. Brown "Analyzing Product Innovations," *Research-Technology Management,* July/August 1987, pp. 60–65.

Gomory, R. E. "From the Ladder of Science to the Product Development Cycle," *Harvard Business Review,* November/December 1989, Vol. 67, pp. 99–105.

Gordon, G. G., N. DiTomaso, and G. F. Farris. "Managing Diversity in R&D Groups," *Research-Technology Management,* January/February 1991, pp. 18–22.

Graves, S. B. "Why Costs Increase When Projects Accelerate," *Research-Technology Management,* March/April 1989, pp. 16–18.

Green, S. G., A. S. Bean, and B. K. Snavely. "What Happens to Ideas?" *Research-Technology Management,* November 1984, pp. 20–23.

Herbert, E. "How Japanese Companies Set R&D Directions," *Research-Technology Management,* September/October 1990, pp. 28–37.

Himmelfarb, P. A. "U. S. Products Must Get to the Marketplace Faster," *The Business Journal,* May 7, 1990.

Holusha, J. "Are We Eating Our Seed Corn?" *The New York Times,* May 13, 1990.

"How Japan Is Beating the Others Cold," *Business Week,* September 3, 1990, p. 79.

"How Japan Lead Inhibits U.S. Project," *The New York Times,* December 18, 1990.

Inman, B. R., and D. F. Burton, Jr. "Technology and Competitiveness: The New Policy Frontier," *Foreign Affairs,* Spring 1990, pp. 116–134.

"Invented in U.S., Spurned in U.S., A Technology Flourishes in Japan," *The New York Times,* December 16, 1990.

Ireland, D. R., M. A. Hitt, and J. Skivington. "Managing R&D in Diversified Companies," *Research-Technology Management,* July/August 1990, pp. 37–42.

"It's a Shakier Perch for Toshiba's Laptops," *Business Week,* August 5, 1991, pp. 62–64.

Kanter, R. M., C. Ingols, E. Morgan, and T. K. Seggerman. "Driving Corporate Entrepreneurship," *Management Review,* Special Report, 1989, pp. 5–7.

Kleinfield, N. R. "Ingersoll-Rand Did the Impossible: Collapsed the Design Cycle to One Year," *The New York Times,* March 25, 1990.

Klimstra, P. D. and J. Potts. "What We've Learned: Managing R&D Projects," *Research-Technology Management,* May/June 1988, pp. 83–93.

Klus, J. P. "Criteria for Success," *Corporate Report Wisconsin,* July 1990, pp. 20–24.

Kuczarski, T. D. "Five Hallmarks of Innovators," *R&D Magazine*, May 1990, p. 155.

Kumar, S., and Y. P. Gupta. "Cross-Functional Teams Improve Manufacturing at Motorola's Austin Plant," *Industrial Engineering*, May 1991, pp. 32–36.

Kuttner, R. "Industry Needs a Better Incubator than the Pentagon," *Business Week*, April 30, 1990.

"Laptops: The Machines Are Tiny, the Potential Is Huge," *Business Week*, March 18, 1991, pp. 118–124.

LaZerte, D. J. "Market Pull/Technology Push," *Research-Technology Management*, March/April 1989, pp. 25–29.

Leet, R. H. "How Top Management Sees R&D," *Research-Technology Management*, January/February 1991, pp. 15–17.

Luckenbach, T. A. "Encouraging 'Little C' and 'Big C' Creativity," *Research-Technology Management*, March 1986, pp. 43–44.

Maccoby, M. "Deming Critiques American Management," *Research-Technology Management*, May/June 1990, pp. 43–44.

Magnusson, P., and N. Gross. "Japan's Latest End-Run Around Free Trade," *Business Week*, October 1, 1990, p. 32.

Markoff, J. "A Corporate Lag in Research Funds Is Causing Worry: High Tech Edge at Stake," *The New York Times*, January 23, 1990.

McCarthy, M. J. "U.S. Companies Shop Abroad for Product Ideas," *The Wall Street Journal*, March 14, 1990.

McCormick, J. "The Vision Thing: Try It, You'll Like It," *Business Month*, May 1990, pp. 66–67.

McGovern, F. "Teaming Up," *USAir Magazine*, March 1991, pp. 41–49.

McGuinness, N. W., and H. A. Conway. "Managing the Search for New Product Concepts: A Strategic Approach," *R&D Management* (UK), October 1989, pp. 297–308.

Miller, R. R. "Do Mergers and Acquisitions Hurt R&D?," *Research-Technology Management*, March/April 1990, pp. 11–15.

Miller, D. B. "Understanding the R&D Culture," *Management Review*, Special Report, 1989, pp. 18–23.

Mower, J. C. "Rewarding Technical Teamwork," *Research-Technology Management*, September/October 1989, pp. 24–29.

Murray, A., and U. C. Lehner. "Strained Alliances: What U.S. Scientists Discover, the Japanese Convert into Profit," *The Wall Street Journal*, June 25, 1990.

Naj, A. J. "Creative Energy: GE's Latest Invention—A Way to Move Ideas from Lab to Market," *The Wall Street Journal*, June 14, 1990.

Naj, A. K. "In R&D, the Next Best Thing to Gut Feel," *The Wall Street Journal*, May 21, 1990.

"New Boeing Airliner Shaped by the Airlines," *The New York Times,* December 9, 1990.

O'Boyle, T. F. "GE's Refrigerator Woes Illustrate the Hazards of Changing a Product," *The Wall Street Journal,* May 7, 1990.

Pascale, R. T. "Strategy: So You Think You've Got a Winning Formula . . .," *Business Month,* October 1990, pp. 38–42.

Passell, P. "America's Position in the Economic Race: What the Numbers Show and Conceal," *The New York Times,* March 4, 1990.

Pennar, K. "Pinning the Blame for the Dip in R&D Budgets," *Business Week,* April 30, 1990.

Perel, M. "Discontinuities and Challenges in the Management of Technology," *Research-Technology Management,* July/August 1990, pp. 7–9.

"Pinning Down Costs of Product Introductions," *The Wall Street Journal,* November 26, 1990.

Pinto, J. I. "How to Keep R&D Projects from Failing," *Inside R&D,* September 13, 1989, pp. 3–4.

Pinto, J. K., and D. P. Slevin. "Critical Success Factors in R&D Projects," *Research-Technology Management,* January/February 1989, pp. 104–108.

Port, O., Z. Schiller, and R. W. King. "A Smarter Way to Manufacture," *Business Week,* April 30, 1990, pp. 110–117.

Power, D. "Linking R&D to Corporate Strategy," *Management Review,* Special Report, 1989, pp. 12–17.

Prestowitz, C. V., Jr. "Japan . . . George Bush, It's Time to Check In," *Business Month,* October 1990, pp. 49–52.

"R&D Slows as Companies Take a Shorter-Term View," *The Wall Street Journal,* June 28, 1990.

Ramirez, A. "What LBO's Really Do to R&D Spending," *Fortune,* March 13, 1989.

Redenbaugh, R. G. "Beware the God of Quality," *Business Month,* June 1990, p. 11.

Reiner, G. "Lessons from the World's Best Product Developers," *The Wall Street Journal,* August 6, 1990.

Root-Bernstein, R. S. "Strategies of Research," *Research-Technology Management,* May/June 1990, pp. 36–41.

Rose, R. L. "Motorola Profit Report Depresses Stock," *The Wall Street Journal,* October 10, 1990.

Rosenbaum, B. L. "How Successful Technical Professionals Achieve Results," *Research-Technology Management,* January/February 1990, pp. 24–26.

Rutigliano, A. J. "Managing the New: An Interview with Peter Drucker," *Management Review,* Special Report, 1989, pp. 8–11.

Sanderson, S. W. "The Consumer Electronics Industry and the Future of American Manufacturing: How the U.S. Lost the Lead," Report of the Economic Policy Institute, Washington, D.C., 1989, pp. 1–48.

Sanger, D. E. "Japan Keeps up the Big Spending to Maintain Its Industrial Might," *The New York Times,* April 11, 1990.

Schmenner, R. W. "The Merit of Making Things Fast," *Sloan Management Review,* Vol. 30, No. 1, Fall 1988.

Schubert, M. A. "Quality Function Deployment: A Means of Integrating Reliability Throughout," Abstract 12th Annual Rocky Mountain Quality Meeting, Denver, CO, June 7–8, 1986.

Shapero, A. "Managing Creative Professionals," *Research-Technology Management,* March 1985, pp. 25–30.

Shepetuk, A. J. "Is Your Product Development Process a Tortoise or a Hare?" *Management Review,* March 1991, pp. 25–27.

"Shorter Product Cycles Become a Top Corporate Objective," *The Wall Street Journal,* February 1, 1990.

Silk, L. "Can U.S. Recover in Electronics?" *The New York Times,* May 4, 1990.

Souder, W. E. "Improving Productivity Through Technology Push," *Research-Technology Management,* March/April 1989, pp. 19–24.

Souder, W. E. "Encouraging Entrepreneurship in the Large Corporation," *Research-Technology Management,* May 1981, pp. 1–5.

Souder, W. E., and T. Mandakovic. "R&D Project Selection Models," *Research-Technology Management,* July/August 1986, pp. 47–53.

Souder, W. E., and V. Padmanabhan. "Transferring New Technologies from R&D to Manufacturing," *Research-Technology Management,* September/October 1989, pp. 38–43.

Szakonyi, R. "101 Tips for Managing R&D More Effectively," *Research-Technology Management,* July/August 1990, pp. 31–36.

Szakonyi, R. "New Product Development Team: Making It Work," *Inside R&D,* September/October 1989, pp. 3–4.

Szakonyi, R. "Critical Issues in Long Range Planning," *Research-Technology Management,* May/June 1989, pp. 28-32.

Tecklenburg, H. "A Dogged Dedication to Learning," *Research-Technology Management,* July/August 1990, pp. 12–15.

"The Brakes Go on in R&D," *Business Week,* July 1, 1991, pp. 24–26.

"The Battle for Europe: Japan Muscles in on the West—and a Shakeout Begins," *Business Week,* June 3, 1991, pp. 44–52.

Uttal, B. "Speeding New Ideas to Market," *Fortune,* March 2, 1987, p. 62.

Vannoy, E. H., and J. A. Davis. "Matrix Management of Reliability Testing," Abstract 14th Annual Rocky Mountain Quality Meeting, Denver, CO, April 15, 1988.

von Hippel, E. "New Product Ideas from 'Lead Users'," *Research-Technology Management,* May/June 1989, pp. 82–96.

Walsh, W. J. "Get the Whole Organization Behind New Product Development," *Research-Technology Management,* November/December 1990, pp. 32–36.

Wilson, T. L. "Don't Let Good Ideas Sit on the Shelf," *Research-Technology Management,* May 1984, pp. 12–19.

Wise, G. "It's a Myth That All Inventions Come from the Outside," *Research-Technology Management,* July/August 1989, pp. 7–8.

Wolff, M. F. "Rules of Thumb for Project Management," *Research-Technology Management: Selected Papers,* 1984–89, pp. 6–8.

Wolff, M. F. "Building Teams—What Works (Sometimes)," *Research-Technology Management,* November/December 1989, pp. 9–10.

Wolff, M. F. "Technology Transfer: A GM Manager's Story," *Research-Technology Management,* September/October 1989, pp. 9–10.

Wolff, M. F. "Before You Try Team Building," *Research-Technology Management,* January/February 1988, pp. 79–81.

Wolff, M. F. "To Innovate Faster, Try the Skunk Works," *Research-Technology Management,* September/October 1987, pp. 72–73.

Wolff, M. F. "Overcoming Roadblocks to Commercializing Industrial R&D Projects," *Research-Technology Management,* July/August 1986, pp. 44–46.

Wolff, M. F. "Picking the Right Technology Should Be First Priority," *Research-Technology Management,* July 1981, pp. 5–6.

Womack, J., D. T. Jones, and D. Roos. "How Lean Production Can Change the World," *The New York Times,* September 23, 1990.

INDEX